W9-APN-806

Beatrix Potter

Twayne's English Authors Series

Kinley E. Roby, Editor

Northeastern University

TEAS 422

BEATRIX POTTER
(1866–1943)
R. J. Thrift, photographer
Reproduced by permission of the
National Trust of the United Kingdom

Beatrix Potter

By Ruth K. MacDonald

New Mexico State University

Twayne Publishers • *Boston*

Beatrix Potter

Ruth K. MacDonald

Copyright © 1986 by G. K. Hall & Co.
All Rights Reserved
Published by Twayne Publishers
A Division of G. K. Hall & Co.
70 Lincoln Street
Boston, Massachusetts 02111

Copyediting supervised by Lewis DeSimone
Book production by Elizabeth Todesco
Book design by Barbara Anderson

Typeset in 11 pt. Garamond
by Compset, Inc., of Beverly, Massachusetts

Printed on permanent/durable acid-free paper
and bound in the United States of America

Library of Congress Cataloging in Publication Data

MacDonald, Ruth K.
    Beatrix Potter.

    (Twayne's English authors series; TEAS 422)
    Bibliography: p.
    Includes index.
    1. Potter, Beatrix, 1866–1943—Criticism and interpretation.
2. Children's stories, English—History and criticism.
3. Animals in literature.
4. Illustration of books—England.
5. Animals in art.
I. Title. II. Series.
PR6031.072Z69   1986   823'.8   85-24829
ISBN 0-8057-6917-X

Contents

About the Author

Ruth K. MacDonald is professor of English at New Mexico State University, where she teaches literature for children. She received her B.A. and M.A. in English from the University of Connecticut, a Ph.D. in English from Rutgers University, and an M.B.A. in business communications from the University of Texas at El Paso. She is past president and treasurer of the Children's Literature Association and has chaired the division of children's literature for the Modern Language Association and the Northeast Modern Language Association. Her book *Literature for Children in England and America, 1646–1774* (Troy, N.Y.: Whitston Press, 1982) is a study of various genres of literature for children in the period. She has also contributed the Twayne United States Authors Series volume *Louisa May Alcott*. She has published a number of articles in various periodicals and dictionaries on both British and American children's literature. She has taught literature for children at Northeastern University, Boston, Massachusetts; the University of California at Los Angeles; Wheaton College, Norton, Massachusetts; and Middlesex County College, Edison, New Jersey.

Preface

This is the first book-length critical study of Beatrix Potter. Any student of Potter owes an incalculable debt to Leslie Linder and Anne Carroll Moore, whose chronicling and documenting of Potter's writing and artwork are the beginning of any such study. Mr. Linder's translation of Potter's secret journal sheds light on a life that, even with his previous work, would have otherwise remained dark and difficult to comprehend. Potter was particularly sensitive to intrusions in her life and resisted any attempts to make her a public personage. But most of the work on Potter to this point has been appreciative rather than critical; complicating the problem is her achievement in two artistic media: print and illustration. Scholars trained in criticizing the one have had little to say about the other, and there has been little investigation into her books as literature or as picture stories, in spite of the attention given to the illustrations as a series of isolated illustrations.

This book seeks to fill the void. I have limited my commentary to the study of Potter's Peter Rabbit series, since that set of twenty-three volumes is the most readily available of her works, and because these stories are the most popular. I have also sought to describe Potter's accomplishments in terms of the tradition that precedes her and that which emanates from her. Above all, I have tried to evaluate her work in both written and visual form, and to relate the functioning of the two to each other. I have paid particular attention to her revisions of her works while they were in preparation, to her sources of inspiration and artistic energy, and to her thematic concerns and development over the course of her career.

This book is divided into five chapters: the first chronicles Potter's life and accomplishments and seeks to elucidate the sources of the tremendous outpouring of her work in the first decade of the twentieth century. The second chapter examines her rabbit books; for convenience, I have also included *The Story of Miss Moppet* in this chapter because its link with *The Story of a Fierce Bad Rabbit* as a panoramic book is stronger than with any other book in Potter's work. The third is a catchall chapter to take in the books about a broad variety of animals over the entire span of her active career. The fourth is an examination of those books inspired by her home in Near Sawrey. And the last contains an evaluation of the sources of her literary longevity. Throughout, my attempt has been to evaluate the language of the works critically and seek out thematic unities across the twenty-three small books. I have also sought to evaluate the pictures as part of a series designed to tell a story and as commentary on the text that accompanies them.

My particular thanks go to the overseers of Potter's property at Hill Top Farm in Near Sawrey for the time they devoted to answering my inquiries. I also am particularly grateful to Michael Pownall for his support during this project.

Ruth K. MacDonald

New Mexico State University

Chronology

1866   Helen Beatrix Potter born London, England, 28 July.

1876   First extant signed sketch, "Foxglove and Periwinkle," 9 February.

1881   Awarded Art Student's Certificate of the Second Grade from the Science and Art Department of the Committee of the Council on Education, 1 July; first dated entry in coded journal, 4 November.

1890   Illustrations for *A Happy Pair* by Frederic Weatherly.

1893   Picture letter containing the original story of *Peter Rabbit* sent to Noel Moore, 4 September; picture letter containing the original story of *Jeremy Fisher* sent to Eric Moore, 5 September.

1894   Picture letter containing the original story of *Little Pig Robinson* sent to Eric Moore, 28 March; visit to Gloucester and inspiration for *The Tailor of Gloucester*, 12 June.

1895   *A Frog He Would a-Fishing Go.*

1897   Last dated entry in coded journal, 31 January; "On the Germination of the Spores of *Agaricineae*" presented before the Linnaean Society, 1 April; picture letter containing the original story of *Squirrel Nutkin* sent to Noel Moore, 28 August.

1901   Picture letter containing the revised story of *Squirrel Nutkin* sent to Norah Moore, 25 September; *The Tale of Peter Rabbit,* first private edition.

1902   *The Tale of Peter Rabbit,* second private edition, February; first Warne edition, December; *The Tailor of Gloucester,* first private edition.

1903   *The Tailor of Gloucester,* Warne edition; *The Tale of Squirrel Nutkin.*

1904   *The Tale of Benjamin Bunny; The Tale of Two Bad Mice.*

1905   Proposal of marriage from Norman Warne received and accepted, 25 July; purchase of Hill Top Farm, Near Sawrey, August; death of Norman Warne, 25 August. *The Tale of Mrs. Tiggy-Winkle; The Tale of the Pie and the Patty-Pan.*

1906   *The Tale of Mr. Jeremy Fisher; The Story of a Fierce Bad Rabbit; The Story of Miss Moppet.*

1907   *The Tale of Tom Kitten.*

1908   *The Tale of Jemima Puddle-Duck; The Roly-Poly Pudding.*

1909   Purchase of Castle Farm, Near Sawrey; *The Tale of the Flopsy Bunnies; Ginger and Pickles.*

1910   *The Tale of Mrs. Tittlemouse.*

1911   *Peter Rabbit's Painting Book; The Tale of Timmy Tiptoes.*

1912   *The Tale of Mr. Tod.*

1913   Marriage to William Heelis, London, 14 October; *The Tale of Pigling Bland.*

1917   *Tom Kitten's Painting Book; Appley Dapply's Nursery Rhymes.*

1918   *The Tale of Johnny Town-Mouse.*

1922   *Cecily Parsley's Nursery Rhymes.*

1923   Purchase of Troutbeck Park.

1925   Beginning of correspondence with Bertha Mahony (Miller) of *The Horn Book; Jemima Puddle-Duck's Painting Book.*

1927   Beginning of fund-raising for The National Trust for Windermere Ferry property through *The Horn Book.*

1928   *Peter Rabbit's Almanac for 1929.*

1929   *The Fairy Caravan.*

1930   *The Tale of Little Pig Robinson.*

1932   *Sister Anne.*

1943   Death of Beatrix Potter, 22 December.

1944   *Wag-by-Wall.*

1955   *The Tale of the Faithful Dove.*

1966   *The Journal of Beatrix Potter.*

Chapter One
The Making of an Artist

Helen Beatrix Potter was born on 28 July 1866, at her parents' home in the Kensington district of London. For most of her first thirty years of life she stayed in the third-floor nursery of the house at Number 2 Bolton Gardens. The first child and only daughter of Helen and Rupert Potter, she was seldom invited downstairs to join her parents for meals and was not permitted beyond the front door without her governess. When she was old enough to go to school, tutors came to supplement the teaching her governesses could give her. Even when her only sibling, Walter Bertram, was born when she was five years old, she remained a solitary child. As soon as he was old enough to go to a boarding school, his parents sent him away. Thus, her childhood was a quiet one, although she herself admitted that she was not unhappy. She was allowed out occasionally to walk about in the public gardens in Kensington, near her home, and sometimes her governesses took her to the new Victoria and Albert Museum being built in Kensington.

Children were only a slight interruption in the lives of deadening regularity that Helen and Rupert Potter led. Both Potters were descended from families who had amassed considerable wealth in running Manchester fabric mills, so there was no need for Mr. Potter to work. Although he was educated in the law, Rupert Potter never practiced his profession. Mrs. Potter's sole responsibility in the house was to direct the many servants that the family could afford. They in turn did the work that might have kept other, less wealthy women occupied. Certainly the Potters could afford all the household help needed to keep them fairly isolated from their children. There seems to have been no thought at Number 2 Bolton Gardens that parents had any responsibility toward their children other than to provide for someone else to take care of them. Most of the time the elder Potters were occupied in trying to find ways to pass the time and invest and spend their considerable wealth.

They did manage to spend considerable time away from Bolton Gardens, both during an extended holiday at Easter and a prolonged summer vacation in the north of England or the south of Scotland. Though the family had money, there seems to have been no interest on anyone's part in visiting any places beyond the shores of England. Even these vacations could be monotonously regular in their locations: for the first twelve years of young Beatrix's life, the family rented Dalguise House in Scotland for three or four months every summer. And the punctuality of meals, carriage rides for Mrs. Potter, and long walks for Mr. Potter was observed as fastidiously on vacation as when the family was in London.

For all that the Potter family was tyrannically ruled by the clock, the vacations provided a genuine release for both Beatrix and her younger brother. Both children were allowed unsupervised walks and adventures into the farmlands and woods surrounding Dalguise House and the other summer homes that the elder Potters rented. There were no tutors to enforce regular school hours, and as long as the children managed to escape from parental supervision, there seems to have been little concern about what they were doing. In this case, children who were not seen and not heard were assumed to be as well-behaved as children who were seen and not heard.

During these escapes from parental regimen both Beatrix and Bertram learned to appreciate the simplicity and rugged endurance of life in the country. They observed farmers and shepherds at work and discovered the pleasures of close observation of the wild, untamed nature of the woods. Both children were avid sketchers and painters, and their walks provided them with much inspiration for further artistic endeavors. Sketchbooks belonging to both children still exist which show their careful recordings of north country specimens of flora and fauna. Occasionally, the children found wild animals and tried to make pets of the smaller creatures. Those who succumbed to the young Potter's blandishments might well find themselves in cages on the train back to London. Those who died or were found already dead were usually sketched and occasionally skinned, boiled down, and reconstructed in skeletal form. In any case, the children found much to absorb their time and energies when they were away from home. It is not surprising that as soon as they could declare their independence, both Beatrix and Bertram chose to return to this remote country to become farmers.

Back at Bolton Gardens, Beatrix was separated from her brother by the time he was seven and she was twelve. She was left to content herself with the companionship of her governesses, tutors, and her pets. Some of these pets were the wild animals brought home from vacation. Others were the rats and mice who lived in the walls. Still others were purchased on those rare outings permitted to Beatrix, when she might go with one of her parents or her governess to a local market. Since the only intrusion from downstairs might well be the meal trays sent up to keep the girl literally in her place, her parents do not seem to have known or cared too much what kind of menagerie she kept in her room. Of course, the occasional snake who left his confines might be a problem if he carelessly made an appearance in the parental chambers, and the frog who jumped out of the window might have made a mess on the pavement below. But as long as neither Beatrix nor her pets made any impression on the elder Potters, what went on upstairs was of little concern to them.

It was from these pets and from the wildlife that she observed and sketched on vacation that Beatrix Potter first began to collect her inspirations for her many animal stories. A warm fire and a plentiful meal might easily persuade an animal to fall asleep in the schoolroom; and an animal asleep makes a good subject to draw. Because she spent so much time isolated and yet unsupervised, young Beatrix had as much time as she wanted to do sketches of her pets in all sorts of positions. When she went to the Museum of Natural History, she took her sketchbook with her and spent many hours, even as a child, studying the skeletons of small animals that were on exhibit. All of this close observation throughout a childhood unnaturally prolonged by parental domineering resulted in an artist uniquely trained to draw animals, not only from life, but also in imaginary situations, perhaps even with clothes on.

This willingness to capture wild animals, either on paper or in a cage, is characteristic of Potter's habit of mind. As a young child untrained about the need for wild animals to remain in their own habitats, she frequently captured them to make them pets, with little consideration as to whether the new home would suit the animals. At times it is clear that she realized her own role in the ill health of some of them. For instance, her pet hedgehog, Mrs. Tiggy-Winkle, approached old age with increasingly failing health. Potter herself admitted that the hedgehog's decline was at least partly her doing: ". . . I am a little afraid that the long course of unnatural diet and indoor life is beginning to tell on her. It is a wonder she has lasted so long."[1] Though she recognized that human food might be injurious to the health of her pets, yet she never hesitated to dose her animals with medication for humans. Her irreverence for nature as she found it is evident not only in her treatment of animals, but also in her attitude toward antiquities and geological formations. As she said in her journal when, at age twenty-nine she went with a family friend to view some fossils recently excavated, "I beg to state I intend to pick up everything I find which is not too heavy."[2]

This willingness to intrude herself on nature was part of her need to master her surroundings, to exert what little power and possession she could, given that her parents were determined to keep her powerless and impoverished. Part of this control could be exerted in her drawing. As she noted in a journal entry for 4 October 1884, her habit of mind led her constantly to draw what she saw: "It is all the same, drawing, painting, modelling, the irresistible desire to copy any beautiful object which strikes the eye. Why cannot one be content to look at it? I cannot rest, I must draw, however poor the result . . ." (106). When later in her life she settled down to live in the country, both her children's stories, set more and more frequently among wild animals, and her own personal habits changed. She could admire nature without intruding herself upon it or destroying it. But until that point in her life where she felt herself in control, the reader of her journal and student of her work notes this willingness to destroy, by dissection or disruption, the nature she found around her, to sacrifice it in the pursuit of her art or ownership.

Art Training

Art, especially painting, seems to have been the one real hobby that the elder Potters pursued. They were intimate friends with Sir John Millais, a famous painter of his time, and were at least passing acquaintances with James Whistler, whose *Study in Black and Grey* is now more familiarly known as "Whistler's Mother." Mr. Potter purchased some of the original drawings that Randolph Caldecott had made for children's books and hung them in his daughter's schoolroom. By the time she was in her teens, Beatrix was allowed to accompany her parents on their visits to various art exhibitions, and the secret journal that she began keeping in 1881 gives a record of her careful evaluations of each painting that she saw at various exhibits. Though the observations are at first not terribly informative, yet by the time she was in her twenties, she reveals herself as an acute and careful critic of the artwork she saw around her.

In her teens Beatrix began to consider art less as simply a diversion and more as a discipline to keep both mind and hand busy during her long hours on the third floor. At age eleven she began to sign or initial those drawings or paintings that she considered finished and worthy. So even at this early age she saw a professional commitment for herself in art. By age twelve her parents allowed her special tutors for art lessons. The only objections they seem to have shown to this artistic pursuit were lodged when the daughter either spent too much time on her drawing or wanted lessons that the parents considered too expensive. Though she objected to some of her lessons as being too confining for her own style of painting, yet she is not without influence on her art. Janet Adam Smith has likened her landscapes to Constable's in their "dewey freshness."[3] Even Potter herself admitted to modeling her early children's books after Randolph Caldecott's, from which artist she inherited a sense of the possible uses of color in the lithographic process by which both artists saw their books reproduced. Like Caldecott and his contemporaries Walter Crane and Kate Greenaway, Potter also set her children's books in some past period, usually the early nineteenth-century Regency. In the case of her later books, all seem to have an antique flavor not because she was deliberately setting them in another time, but because she was drawing the country life around her in Sawrey, where life was little changed from the previous century. Thus she deliberately chose a setting both realistic and archaic; one suspects that its dated quality was part of its appeal for Potter.

All three of Potter's artistic forebears set a new standard for detailed and careful draftsmanship in their artwork for children's books, and Caldecott especially established himself as the master of the detailed background, filling in the story or rhyme by giving it specificity of setting and time even when the story itself was not forthcoming with such details. Greenaway's costuming of her children is particularly noteworthy, for although Potter did not share her concern for child figures in her pictures, she did share Greenaway's concern for historical veracity in costuming her animals. The legacy that Greenaway left to Potter is particularly clear in *The Tailor of Gloucester*. Potter's whole story evolves around a particular Regency period tailcoat and waistcoat, which she modeled after specimens she found in the clothing collection at the Victoria and Albert Museum. Crane's elegantly devised page, with illuminated capitals and carefully designed scrollwork gave Potter a sense of the page as a limited space for her artwork. And his *Baby's Opera*, with its nursery rhymes that Potter grew up reading, clearly influenced her own propensity to rhyme and riddle in her writings.

In terms of her animal characters, Potter's greatest debt is to Thomas

Bewick, the wood engraver of the late eighteenth century. Bewick's animal figures show his observation of accurate detail, much like Potter's own work with skeletons and microscopes, in order to master the intricacies of animal form. Bewick also showed a new interest in the design of the page, with vignettes, or circular white space, framing the animal figure, much as Potter does in *Peter Rabbit*. Bewick's animals, like Potter's, are not simply figures against an empty background, but rather are shown living in their natural habitats, framed by native flora and fauna. No artist of Potter's time or before paid as much careful attention to animals in nature as had Bewick, and Potter inherits from him a sense of veracity in nature study.

There were other childhood influences on Potter's adult writing style. Her debt to the Uncle Remus stories of Joel Chandler Harris is clearest in her books about rabbits and foxes, either separately or in combination. Though Peter Rabbit is not Br'er Rabbit, he does bear some resemblance to him, and the foxes in *Jemima Puddle-Duck* and *Mr. Tod* are modeled after the mannerly plantation gentleman known in Chandler's stories as Br'er Fox. The clearly articulated animosity between species, as seen in Harris's stories, became a prominent feature of Potter's stories as well. She also read many fairy tales and found particularly appealing those that had animal characters. In her twenties, when she was casting around for a life's occupation, she recalled Aesop's fables, again childhood favorites because of the many animals in them that are characterized by their species: Aesop's sheep are sheepish, his foxes sly, his dogs loyal but also sometimes lazy. Though she also had available works by Maria Edgeworth, Walter Scott, Edward Lear, and Lewis Carroll, her favorites and most-remembered were those with animals in them, and later, she drew on them for possible publishing projects.

As she grew up, Potter became more interested in leading her own life and working with her art, both written and visual, independent of her family. Yet her parents, especially her mother, came to expect that their daughter would take over the handling of household affairs. Mr. Potter began to suffer from some nervous disorders that he claimed were exacerbated when his daughter failed to attend to him. As they grew older, the Potter parents came to demand more and more of their daughter's time and interest. During her teens and twenties she tried to comply with their demands, but by her late twenties she clearly could not be the obedient daughter in the strict and sometimes demeaning terms in which her parents defined that role. She persevered in her desire, recorded in her journal for 3 March 1883, to "do something" (30), to find some purpose and definition to her life apart from her parents' insistence that she was no more than an extension of them and even an embarrassment to them. She needed some discipline to order her existence, which she later found in her publishing.

There seem to have been few quarrels between parents and daughter during her adolescence and young womanhood, but Potter's rebellion about the kind of life her parents forced upon her did surface in two ways. First, during her late teens she became mysteriously ill, perhaps with rheumatic fever, and in any case enervated to the point of near-paralysis. Her parents took such drastic measures as cutting off all her hair and dosing her with a variety of noxious medications ordered by doctors. The illness did no permanent damage to her health, but the source of the illness is curiously unexplained except as a kind of female complaint of unspecified origin, the nervous reaction to a nerve-wracking life.

The Secret Journal

Potter also showed her desire for more independence in the secret-code journal that she kept intermittently from her thirteenth or fourteenth through thirtieth years. The journal records insights and observations that for the most part are quotidian and unexceptional. When she first started writing, she seems to have recorded a number of jokes, as if storing up a repertoire to use in social situations when the conversation lagged. The most exceptional aspect of the diary is the miniscule code writing in which she insisted on recording her thoughts. The code is not a complicated one, although it did frustrate its decoder, Leslie Linder, for a number of years. It is a simple substitution of one letter for another, with a few abbreviations for common words and letter combinations. The hand in which Potter wrote is so small that an average-sized page of paper might include a thousand words, sometimes as many as fifteen hundred on a large sheet. The fluency with which she wrote in code betrays her easy familiarity with her system. It appears to have been no more complicated for her than other, more conventional longhand writing. And yet she chose this meticulous, complicated system to record information that would only rarely have been offensive to her parents.

Perhaps she decided to write in code because it afforded her some of the only privacy of thought she knew in her life; her parents were certainly domineering, becoming more so as they sensed their daughter's growing maturity and independence. Perhaps she used the code simply as an exercise to keep her occupied and untouched by the stultifying boredom that might otherwise have depressed her spirits. It may be that paper was rationed on the third floor, especially as the elder Potters saw that artwork was luring their daughter away from them. Without sufficient paper she could not draw, and so to keep the daughter attentive, they denied her the materials that might distract her from them. She therefore used the paper sparingly, recording as much as she could on one precious sheet.

It is also possible that with such small handwriting the notes became nearly invisible, certainly not worth the effort to look carefully at the fine print. In any case, in the journal the reader sees very little of Beatrix Potter as a person, especially in the early years, although one senses the presence around her that would have encouraged her to resort to such a secretive form of communication, if only with herself. One also sees an artist practicing the discipline of drawing the minute. Though it is difficult to say that the handwriting presages the small books to come, yet the smallness and ease of the handwriting were a kind of practice for the care with which she later executed her drawings for her books.

If the journal does not give much sense of what Beatrix Potter was like as an adolescent and young woman, it does paint a vivid portrait of her habits and quality of mind. She was keenly observant of small details around her, especially and not surprisingly of the animals she saw on her infrequent expeditions. For example, in 1881 Rupert Potter took his daughter to tour a silver manufacturing plant in London. While she was there, Potter took in not only the explanations of how the processing of silver worked and how the machinery functioned, but also the plenitude of cats in the factory, nearly one in every room (4 November 1881, 2–6). Her journal is filled with observations of animals and children, all probably overlooked by her companions, but of interest and importance to her.

Potter also seems to have had an exceptional memory. Though it is possible that she had catalogs from various art exhibitions that she visited, it is equally likely that she remembered, in order of their presentation in the exhibit, every picture and her reaction to each. Her unusually good memory is apparent in two other journalistic habits: first, her apparent word-for-word transcription of conversations, especially those of her grandmother, and, second, her habit of recording how many plays by Shakespeare she had memorized. During her teens and early twenties she set herself the task of memorizing whole plays, scene by scene. Though in the journal she graded herself as to how much of and how well she knew each play, yet by age twenty-eight she reckoned that she had mastered six of them in the past year. The plays do not seem to indicate any particular taste on her part for the various kinds of plays Shakespeare wrote, but rather an eclectic, wide-ranging, perhaps even undiscriminating desire to master these works. She also remembered and recorded from nearly perfect memory parts of the Bible, especially the Psalms. When, later in her life, she was asked what she did to perfect her writing, she responded, "My usual way of writing is to scribble, and cutout, and write it again and again. The shorter and plainer the better. And read the Bible (unrevised version and Old Testament) if I feel my style wants chastening."[4] The meticulous habits that she practiced on her published works and unidentifiable influences on those works seem obvious from the journal that she thought no one would ever read.

Potter also shows a keen interest in her grandmother Crompton and records her pleasure in visiting her grandparents' home at Camfield Place, Hertfordshire. Potter's early interest, even as a small child, in her grandmother's stories of her own youth and her keen appreciation of the old house and its antiques early marked her as one misplaced in history. She was always interested in old things, almost without regard to the extent of their agedness. As in her books, she shows in her journal her love of earlier historical periods, when life apparently seemed to have been better than what she was experiencing. She became a collector, not only of her grandmother's reminiscences, which she remembered with surprising accuracy, but also of antiques, especially porcelain and pottery. This desire not only to acquire and remember old things but also to live the life of an earlier time is clear in her books. Her choice to live in the isolated village of Near Sawrey when she was finally free to choose a home for herself, in a place where life truly was unchanged from the last century, further illustrates this desire to live the life of an earlier historical period.

The journal shows that Beatrix Potter was not only an illustrator, she was also a writer. Though she recorded in her journal her compulsion to paint, to record what she saw on paper, her records are not only visual, they are also verbal. It is difficult to say that there is a direct Shakespearean influence on her writing style, or that her cadence and rhythms clearly reflect the sonorous poetry and Anglo-Saxon diction of the King James Bible. In fact, the clearest influence on her writing is her childhood nursery rhymes, from which she derived a highly alliterative style. But her desire to capture the precise words used by someone in casual conversation, her willingness to exert herself to the lengths of extended memorization, her attention even to her tiny handwriting, all indicate a fascination not only with how words look on the page, but also how they sound. This careful attention to the exact word in the exact situation later led to lengthy correspondence and arguments with her publishers. But in the journal the reader sees the writer in training to produce the one and only precise word that intuition says is correct.

In the journal there is some sense of depression about the kind of life she led and her increasing exasperation with her parents' tyrannical quirks and compulsions. The initial reaction of the girl in her teens seems to have been simple acceptance and regret that situations seemed unnecessarily difficult and complicated. In her twenties she gradually came to see that her parents were unfairly manipulating her, and finally she came to show her resentment, both in thought and in action, of their control of her. Where she initially said little about their travel arrangements and the cumbersome business of living out of hotels for four months a year, she gradually realized that her parents allowed her the privilege of taking care of the voluminous luggage not to reward her responsibility but to be rid of the burden themselves. She early longed for the permanency and stability of a home, though she did not then protest her parents' frequent trips, and when she finally acquired a house of her own, she furnished it with the kinds of antique belongings that her grandparents chose for Camfield. The years in which she published continued to be times of difficulty and friction between parents and daughter, more clearly and vociferously articulated as time passed. Yet until her marriage at age forty-seven, she always tried to be an obedient daughter, at least as far as her heroic efforts at obedience allowed.

At the time of the journal entries, which she apparently ceased to maintain at about age thirty, she records her delight with the country in the Lake District and the pleasure she found in living there. When she visited Sawrey on her family's summer vacation in 1896, she exclaimed to herself, "It is as nearly perfect a little place as I ever lived in, and such nice old-fashioned people in the village" (422). Though the family had stayed in the same area on previous vacations, never before had Potter so clearly expressed her pleasure in the simple country lifestyle she found there.

It is not surprising that in 1905, after she had published seven books and had derived some independent wealth from her royalties, she bought a farm in Near Sawrey. Though her official excuse to her parents for spending her money was that the farm was a good investment, an explanation to which the elder Potters could have found little to take exception, in reality, the farm was a kind of escape from the rigidity of her life with her parents in London. Her parents frequently objected to her taking time away from them to attend to farm matters, yet she took every opportunity she could to get away. Here she found satisfaction for her desire for a permanent home and a space that was hers alone, to be ordered and controlled as she wished. Though the house was a small one, she clearly articulated in her earlier journal entries her preference for the small and cozy space filled with antiques, a space not unlike the ones she fantasized for her animals. Here was her own version of a rabbit hole, her own neat and orderly place, from which she could bar intruders and limit visitors as she pleased.

Publishing Career

Until she could officially and permanently move away from her parents, Potter also found an escape in London by visiting the home of her last governess, Annie Carter Moore. When Miss Carter first arrived in Bolton Gardens as Potter's governess, she was ostensibly hired to teach German and maintain the surveillance that the parents required over their daughter. But Potter was eighteen, and Carter twenty. Thus the rigid separation of governess and pupil dissolved into the friendship of companions. When Carter left Bolton Gardens two years later to become Mrs. Moore, the friendship between the two young women continued. Mrs. Potter tried to sabotage her daughter's efforts to visit the Moore household in the London suburb of Wandsworth by being indecisive as to whether the carriage would be available. Still, the daughter did manage regular visits.

As offspring arrived to crowd the household, Beatrix found in the Moore home a relaxed and casual attitude toward family relations that hardly characterized her own home. She also found the pleasure and chaos of youthful high spirits which in her own home rarely saw expression. The Moores were not as obsessed with regularity and punctuality as were the Potters; and young Miss Potter found in the family a much more intimate, if also more disorganized, way of living as a family.

In the Moore family Potter also had her first real experience with children. Her family had few close friends; indeed, there seem to have been few visitors of any age. Potter had few friends of her own, and apparently none who had children. In another time, there would have been various social functions during which a young lady of means would have been introduced to people of her own age with whom she could socialize. But the Potters did not seem to belong to any particular social set, so their daughter was not introduced to potential friends, or perhaps more important, potential marriage partners. Therefore, it is not surprising to find Potter particularly observant of the Moore children as strange and yet delightful phenomena.

Her relationship to the children is not quite clear. Her manner with them was somewhat straight-jacketed by the extremely formal etiquette that prevailed in her time. Her lack of exposure to social situations complicated her sense of appropriate behavior around children. Perhaps the children did not recognize that Potter was an awkward and introverted person. It is difficult to know why she was so particularly attentive to the Moore children and why the children reported in later years that they so much enjoyed her visits. It is as likely that they found her gifts as pleasurable as her presence. In any case, she began a correspondence with the children and maintained it through many more exchanges of letters than have been preserved in Potter archives. These letters usually contained stories and pictures to illustrate them, sometimes anecdotes about her activities while on vacation, usually apologies for not having come to visit. It is not clear whether the children wrote letters back; certainly none have been preserved.

In 1893, when Annie Moore's first child, Noel, became ill with scarlet fever, a visit from Potter was clearly out of the question. Not only might it have been an imposition on the already busy mother of the brood, but Potter's own family was unnaturally fearful of germs, as if disease, like lower social status, might be caught from undesirables. So instead of visiting Noel, as she might have done in different circumstances, Potter decided to write him a letter.

The opening line of the letter, which later developed into *The Tale of Peter Rabbit,* is indicative of the distance that Potter felt between herself and children, even though at the same time she was more at ease with children than with adults: "I don't know what to write to you, so I shall tell you a story of four little rabbits. . . ."[5] Though children were much easier to meet and talk with than adults, still they were not creatures with whom Potter had lived intimately. They were human and could talk back and ask uncomfortable questions. Throughout her life Potter was both familiar with and aloof from children. As her cousin later reported, Potter was content to observe the children and to test out her stories on them, but she did not interact with them as an equal.[6] Though she could engage children in her own stories, and her own imaginative constructs would delight them both, yet she was never entirely accepting of human beings, no matter what their age. As long as they entered her world on her terms, the situation was manageable. However, it is not entirely clear that Potter was really as familiar and comfortable with children as some reports have implied.

In any case, the story, in shortened form and with a false start at the story of Benjamin Bunny waywardly included, was sent to Noel and enjoyed so much by the Moore children that they required that Miss Potter continue to send them picture-story-letters at every opportunity. There is no way of telling how many of these stories were lost because the children read them to shreds or simply misplaced them. But scholars do know that at least four of the books in the Peter Rabbit series had their beginnings in letters to the young Moores: *Peter Rabbit, Benjamin Bunny, Squirrel Nutkin,* and *Jeremy Fisher.* Though Noel was only five years old at the time, he continued to enjoy the letter and preserved it, so that when, in 1901, Miss Potter asked him if he still had it and if he would lend it to her, he could answer yes and comply with the request.

She had been encouraged in her twenties to pursue more actively her interest in fungi, but no one seemed to take seriously the work of an untrained artist, a woman, no less, and an uneducated scientist. In 1897 she had even prepared a paper, "On the Germination of the Spores of the *Agaricineae,*" which was read to the Linnaean Society of London and in which her hypotheses, though not widely accepted at the time, were later proven correct. But the reading of the paper, by proxy, since women were not allowed to present papers, virtually ended her pursuit of a career in fungi, so discouraged had she become at her work's reception. Potter had done some designs for greeting cards, but the scope of such work was too small, it had to be done according to the publisher's specifications and was not at all to her taste about animals in fantasy or in reality, and the task was unsatisfying in terms of literary creativeness. In 1890 she had illustrated a poem by Frederic E. Weatherly, more famous for his lyrics to "The Roses of Picardy" than for his poem "A Happy Pair," which Potter illustrated. Ernest Nister issued a pamphlet called "A Frog He Would a-Fishing Go" (1895), an early prototype of *Jeremy Fisher,* with nine Potter drawings. The idea of writing and drawing for children was not a new one to Potter. When in 1900 a friend of the family suggested that she might do something in the way of a small book for children, she recalled, as does the isolated mind not filled with the chaos of ordinary living, the letter of seven years earlier and thought she might try to use Peter as a story.

When, at first, publishers showed no interest in her book, she decided to publish it herself, using the money from her greeting cards and from a small gift from her father. The result was attractive enough for her to try one publisher again, Frederick Warne and Company, the only house that had shown any polite, if only slight, interest. The firm was known for its list of "healthy literature at popular prices," as the publishers' historians characterize it,[7] and had published the works of Kate Greenaway, Randolph Caldecott, and Edward Lear. The meeting of author and publishers was a felicitous one, for the firm had proven its ability to reproduce subtle watercolors in a quality format and yet, like Potter, preferred to keep prices low. In printed form Potter's book was good enough for the publishers to offer a contract, with the proviso that the text be pruned—Benjamin Bunny's story was to be omitted, saved for another book, the number of pictures reduced from forty-one to thirty-two, and all of them colored, the pen-and-ink sketches being considered unpopular among children's book buyers at the time. Potter willingly complied, though she admitted her doubts about the values of rabbit brown and lettuce green to be interesting enough. The result was the nursery classic *The Tale of Peter Rabbit,* nearly the same as we know it today, which has been translated into several foreign languages, so that its popularity stretches far beyond the English-reading public.

While Potter was seeing the finishing touches on *Peter Rabbit,* she was also busy on another book that she had decided to publish on her own. *The Tailor of Gloucester* was inspired by a story she had heard on one of her rare excursions away from home without her parents. In 1894, one of Potter's cousins invited her to visit her family home near Gloucester. Not only was Potter introduced to her cousin's rather stridently feminist opinions on this trip, but she also heard a local legend about a tailor whose work was finished for him in the night by fairies. The truth of the legend lay in the tailor's apprentices wanting to do their master a favor and working late to finish the waistcoat, but the story about fairy intervention had taken hold in the town, and Potter clearly perceived the story's possibilities if the fairies were changed to mice. Both Potter and her cousin went to visit this tailor's establishment, and Potter insisted on interrupting their holiday excursion to do sketches of the tailor's shop and the streets around it. The idea of a Christmas story was already evident in her mind, for, though she was sketching in the bright sun of a hot summer's day, her drawings transformed the shop and the streets into snowy winter scenes. While touring, she also made sketches of Gloucester Cathedral and the interiors of many local cottages; later at her cousin's house, she posed the son of the family's coachman before the fire in the typical tailor's squat and sketched him, too.

When she went back to London, these sketches remained in her files. When it seemed that the first little book was likely to be a commercial success, being too timid to approach the publishers about another project, she decided to do with the Gloucester story what she had done with *Peter Rabbit:* publish the story herself, in a private edition. This second book was not nearly so little as *Peter Rabbit.* In fact, it was both larger in size and longer, the story more involved, with fewer pictures. The story was originally a Christmas gift for Freda Moore, given to her in 1901, and published in a private edition in 1902.

When the Warne publishing house finally asked about another project, *The Tailor of Gloucester* was already at hand, and with some judicious cutting Warne published it the next year. With the commercial successes of both *Peter Rabbit* and *The Tailor of Gloucester* a matter of record, it became clear to the publishers that Potter could be a gold mine for the firm. In 1903 and for nearly ten years after Warne regularly published one or, more frequently, two Potter books a year, keeping both publishers and author happy and busy.

Norman Warne

Though Potter originally directed her correspondence with her publishers to the company generally, by 1902 she began to rely primarily on Norman Warne, the youngest brother of the family firm, for editorial direction. Norman Warne was not only the youngest of his brothers, he was also the only bachelor among them. He worked carefully and tactfully with Potter, and she valued his opinion highly and nearly always took his advice. It was he who encouraged her to perfect her own style of illustration, rather than imitating Caldecott, her early inclination. Gradually he steered her away from her reliance on nursery rhymes to the careful crafting of her own stories. Through close collaboration and long correspondence, both author and publisher became increasingly familiar with each other. After an acquaintance of three years, Norman Warne finally proposed marriage to Potter, though his shyness about doing so may be the reason for his proposal by mail, while the Potters were on vacation during the summer of 1905.

The couple's meeting was a particularly fortuitous event; certainly the Potter parents did everything they could to discourage their daughter from ever meeting any young men by limiting her funds, time, and means of travel. They did not approve of their daughter going into business as an author-illustrator, for work was something that no man of their social class did without besmirching his reputation as truly upper-class. For a daughter in the family to do so was even more unthinkable. Though sons might have to work on occasions of extreme financial exigency, daughters, like wives, were to remain at home, overseeing the running of the household and pursuing hobbies perhaps, but never abandoning their status as amateurs to pursue any goal professionally, and certainly never for money.

That Beatrix Potter was gradually making enough money to become financially independent was threatening enough to her parents, who expected their daughter to remain always dependent and attentive. That she had entered into this new pursuit expressly against their wishes was a sign that she was becoming increasingly intractable and independent in her thinking. That this new pursuit also introduced her to inferior tradesmen, as the elder Potters considered publishers to be, was horrifying. That she should be a welcome guest in the Warne home was shocking. That she should consider marriage to such a tradesman was, literally, beyond words. The young lady that the Potters had kept so consistently stunted in the role of obedient child was apparently growing up and making up her own mind about what she would do and with whom she would associate. The idea of marriage to Norman Warne was apparently so painful a topic that neither daughter nor parents could discuss the issue with any equanimity. So, when, while the family was on its annual summer holiday in 1905, Beatrix received both the letter of proposal and an engagement ring, her changed status was ignored by the parents and not mentioned by the daughter.

By this time in the history of their relationship Potter and Norman Warne had worked on five books together and were in the process of preparing for publication several more. Potter had spent considerable time in the Warne household, playing with Norman Warne's many nieces and nephews. When Norman Warne built a dollhouse for one of his nieces as a Christmas gift, Potter remarked that it seemed an appropriate home for a family of mice. Thus came the inspiration for *The Tale of Two Bad Mice* (1904). In directing the progress of the book Norman Warne was almost as much the author as Potter herself. Had Mrs. Potter been more cooperative about letting her daughter sketch the house at the Warne home, the romance between Potter and Warne might have developed more rapidly. But perhaps this is exactly what Mrs. Potter feared, and so she forbade further visits. Her daughter had to be content with photographs of the dollhouse for her sketches. However, when Potter requested a glass house for her mice so that she might see inside their nests to observe them more closely, Norman Warne built it for her, and when she needed dolls as models for two characters in the book, he purchased them for her.

Though their intimacy grew primarily through their correspondence, Norman Warne was perhaps the only person in her life who encouraged Potter to write, draw, and publish. His advice to her, as seen in the correspondence that the Warne Company still has between editor and author, was unfailingly sound and did much to shape her sense of the audience for her words and the most suitable execution of drawings for reproduction. She took his advice remarkably well, especially for a woman who was just learning to be an independent thinker. Certainly she would argue a point if she felt strongly about it, but in lesser matters she deferred to Norman Warne's advice, and her books are the better for it.

Though the two were happy for a time, what would probably have been a long and happy life together was abruptly cut short when Norman Warne died of leukemia in August 1905, only two weeks after the engagement and while Potter was still away with her parents on vacation. Symptoms of the disease came on suddenly, and Potter had no idea that her fiancé was dying, so the shock of the news was even greater. Her parents' disapproval of the match and grim satisfaction over the failure of the marriage to come about meant that Potter's grief had no outlet, and so she mourned in silence. Her only confidante was Norman Warne's unmarried sister, Millie, who understood and shared her own grief with Potter.

Hill Top Farm

Increasingly, Beatrix Potter found solace in her work and in her farm in Near Sawrey, which she had purchased, also in the summer of 1905. Though publicly explained as a good investment, privately Potter must have hoped to move to the farm, for she established living quarters for herself there. As usual, her parents tried to limit their daughter's visits to the farm, but she became more and more resourceful about taking trips to oversee her financial holdings. Potter continued to publish books for Warne, though her time was increasingly occupied with trips between Near Sawrey and London, and with the many decisions involved in renovating the farmhouse and turning the farm into a thriving business proposition. Luckily, the farm became an inspiration for her, and the Warne publishing company could rely on Potter to produce in spite of the demands on her time.

It is with the purchase of the house that Potter's most active and most creative period began. Certainly her activity was generated in part by her wish to put behind her the grief over Norman Warne's death. But the purchase of the house gave her the ideal, personal space, the cozy, simple home life that she had longed for since her teens. Her growing self-confidence in her art is evident by the increasingly complex plots she undertook and the strident manner in which she began to talk to her publishers. Norman Warne she considered an arbiter of taste; but she increasingly rebelled against his older brothers' prudery and what she considered their overaccommodating attitude toward public mores. By 1905 her books for Warne show her growing interest in the lives of the farmers and shepherds in her new home in Near Sawrey, and her willingness to write about these lives, in spite of the meddling by her publishers.

Beginning with *The Pie and The Patty-Pan* (1905) and ending with *The Tale of Pigling Bland* (1913), nearly all of Potter's books are set in that remote country village and celebrate the lives of both the farm animals and the people she had become familiar with there. Though Potter continued to publish two books a year until 1910, her attention turned more and more to her farm and to acquiring other farms in the area. The books became a means of expressing her pleasure in her life as a farmer, and a means of financing that lifestyle and preserving it by keeping the land out of the hands of other, more mercenary, absentee owners.

Marriage

In the course of her land acquisitions she dealt primarily with one law firm, whose principal associate was a bachelor attorney of her own age. When William Heelis of Ambleside, a village not far from Near

Sawrey, proposed marriage to Potter in 1912, Potter did not hesitate to accept the proposal nor to defy her parents. One remarkable outcome of her short but decisive argument with her parents was that her brother Bertram revealed that several years earlier he himself had married a farmer's daughter from Ancrum, and had been living happily with her all those years, without the parents' knowledge. Most likely, his sister had been his confidante in the matter. So when the parents sought the son's support in their battle to keep their daughter single, they were unpleasantly surprised. The parents were routed, and Beatrix Potter married William Heelis in the London church of St. Mary Abbott on 14 October 1913. She abruptly and finally moved out of her room on the third floor of her parents' home, to return to Bolton Gardens only rarely. In later life she called the house in Kensington "my unloved birthplace"[8] and showed no regret when it was destroyed by bombs during World War II.

Her marriage not only marked a change in her address; it also ended a period of extraordinary literary and artistic productivity. In her journal entry for 12 June 1894, during the same trip to Gloucester that she heard the story inspiring *The Tailor of Gloucester,* she commented on her cousin's uncomplimentary evaluation of marriage: "I hold an old-fashioned notion that a happy marriage is the crown of a woman's life" (313). Apparently, her ideas of marriage did not change in the intervening years.

She always maintained what H.L. Cox identified as an "amateur" attitude toward her artwork.[9] She published to keep busy and to make money, but she did not see it as her real career, which was marriage and, later, farming. After her marriage Warne could only get her to rewrite projects that she had already started in earlier years, but that had been left aside in favor of other books more nearly finished and ready for publication. The older she became, the more likely she was to complain that her eyesight would not permit her to do the close drawing that her earlier books had required. She also reminded her publishers about the various concerns of the farm that would have to take precedence over any request they made of her for more books. Thus, she would go back to her files and pull out sketches already done and simply touch them up for publication.

Only for *Johnny Town-Mouse* (1918) did she embark on a whole new set of drawings, and the message of the book is a clear defense of her country way of life and avoidance of all that her earlier publishing career in London had meant in terms of disrupting her life. More commonly, she drew a new picture only if it were for interpolation into a set of drawings already finished and earlier laid aside. At one point, she even encouraged the Warnes to hire Ernest A. Aris, whom she considered to be an unbridled copyist of her style, to illustrate *The Story of The Sly Old Cat,* posthumously published in 1971 because she would not prepare the drawings herself. She considered that his imitation of her style was good enough that he could be a sort of pseudo-Beatrix Potter without compromising the quality of her books.[10]

Potter did continue to publish books with Warne, for her lifestyle as a farmer and acquisitive landowner depended on her royalties to make further land purchases possible. This is not to say that she settled down in later years to seclusion and idle retirement. As if she had been waiting all her life for the opportunities that marriage would bring, she turned to life with her country-lawyer husband with a newfound physical energy. She became an accomplished farmer in her fifties; in her sixties she became a champion breeder of Herdwick sheep, a hardy variety which could survive the brutal winters in the hills of the Lake District. Also in this period she became an active member of the National Trust and sought both funds and properties to preserve as open spaces for later generations. Though her literary works are part of her legacy, one cannot underestimate the influence she had on the landscape of England in her tireless efforts to preserve the environment and the older way of life she loved. At her death on 22 December 1943, she willed all her property to the National Trust, including the house that she preserved in her literature.

During her marriage Potter strove to remain anonymous from her reading public. In fact, she would not let her publisher refer inquiries to her directly, and the rumor was widely circulated that Miss Potter was dead. The rumor was at least partly true, for Miss Potter became Mrs. Heelis, and she herself made no reference to her former spinster state or her books. She herself "turned her back"[11] on her former life and devoted herself entirely to her marriage and her farming. Potter somewhat shortsightedly concluded that her public was no longer interested in her writing, since no one inquired about her. Her loathing of notoriety was the result of the intrusiveness of English visitors. Many assumed a familiarity that she found presumptuous. Others treated her as yet another holiday sight to be consumed during their summer vacations. So Potter remained aloof from a public that was otherwise perfectly willing to render the respectful adoration she required.

When an American bookshop owner wrote to inquire about the genesis of her creation, Potter perceived that her admirer was no common tourist, but one who took children's literature seriously, as Potter felt her work deserved. The result of this initial contact with Bertha Mahony of Boston's Women's Educational and Industrial Union was continued correspondence and increased appreciation of Potter's work from Americans. In fact, Potter realized that the American public was a lucrative market. When she found that her special project, the National Trust's development of open-space property in the Lake District, needed money to buy more farms, she wrote to Mahony, now the editor of *Horn Book,* sending along a set of sketches drawn after the original Peter Rabbit pictures, to be sold for the benefit of this purchase. Potter continued her correspondence and frequent visits with touring Americans. As a result, she resumed writing and sketching, though not drawing and painting, an important distinction in terms of her earlier close, careful work, in order to produce some books to be published exclusively in the United States. *The Fairy Caravan* (1929) was admittedly not Potter's best work—perhaps because she found it less satisfactory, more fantastic, less compact, and less true to the animal natures that had early dominated her successful writings. She permitted the book to be published only in Philadelphia by David McKay, in an arena where perhaps more discriminating eyes would not read it. By the time that Potter had published this book exclusively with David McKay, the publishing house of Frederick Warne, long her supporter and sole outlet for her books, insisted that they, too, share in the rare event of a new book from their most requested author. *Little Pig Robinson* was published simultaneously in Philadelphia and London in 1930, and its author's reputation, rather than its literary value, sustained its sales on both sides of the Atlantic. Bertha Mahony also requested a book for her American readers. She was not only editor but also founder of the *Horn Book* magazine, a review of children's books, and a publishing house for related material. With *Wag-by-Wall* (1944) as a long-standing part of the *Horn Book* list, both the magazine and the National Trust benefited from the proceeds.

Potter no longer had the eyes to do the minute illustrations of her middle age, and though she could still tell a good story, the results had none of the energetic freshness of her best works. Only *The Fairy Caravan* is illustrated by Potter, with colored drawings from her files and pen-and-ink sketches that her eyes still permitted her to do, executed specifically for McKay. She might not be able to do the coloring she had done in her youth, but, as she herself commented, she could still sketch. The few drawings for *Little Pig Robinson* were saved from an earlier period. The stories are longer, less vigorous from lack of the editing and polishing that typified her best works. Without the discipline of the pictures to punctuate the stories, to slow them down, Potter tended to ramble on, with little sense of what was interesting or even well expressed. The pictures were a way for her to focus on her story more clearly, to look at the words as well as the drawings on the page. Without them, she lapsed into unnecessary, occasionally verbose description.

The Tale of the Faithful Dove (1955) was found among her papers after her death and published posthumously, illustrated later by Marie Angel in 1971. Like the works of many older artists, these four last works still show the genius that had earlier made for popularity and artistic success but that no longer burned as energetically. Even though some of the books originated in Potter's great creative period, they did not receive the care and attention the other books of that period had lavished upon them.

Though Potter's early life might have twisted and damaged a personality of lesser strength, for her it provided a period of intense focus and exploration of her abilities. She wrote in later life that her isolation did not make her unhappy and, in fact, preserved much of her originality. Roger Sale points to a change in her illustration when she finally encloses her drawing in some kind of frame; he points to the same effect of the white space surrounding her writing on the printed page.[12] Like the white space around her drawings and words, the blankness of Potter's early life helped her to focus clearly on details, and the purchase of her own kind of personal frame at Hill Top farm released the energies stored during her early life. She learned to fill the blank spaces in her mind with the raw material for her stories. When she found the appropriate outlet for the material, and when she could confine this energy, both within her own home and between the covers of a small book, the result was a remarkable intensity and clarity of vision. Though she gave up publishing after her marriage, she never gave up sketching or writing, as the voluminous files of paintings and letters show. She simply directed her energy elsewhere and found satisfaction in other recipients of her intense observation.

Chapter Two
Peter Rabbit and His Kin

Of all her books *The Tale of Peter Rabbit* and its sequels are Potter's best-known and most successful. Spanning as they do her most active period of writing, a study of them shows the increasing complexities of her plots and characterizations, and increasing daring in her subject matter. The personalities range from a rabbit who is simply naughty to characters who are disagreeable and sinister. Though Peter and his cousin Benjamin remain paired as complementary versions of rabbit nature, they develop from carefree little rabbits to thoughtful adults capable of contemplation and cognition. To complement their growing depth of character, Potter added more complex villains to her other characters in the rabbit stories. While *Peter Rabbit,* her first book, is her best book for very young children, *Mr. Tod,* the last of the rabbit books, written nearly at the end of her writing career, is one of her most complex and successful in plot and tone.

Potter always felt particularly close to rabbits, having lived with them early on as pets and having observed them closely. The nature of her assessment of them is obvious from her journal: "Rabbits are creatures of warm volatile temperament but shallow and absurdly transparent. It is this naturalness, one touch of nature, that I find so delightful . . ." (300). Given their shallowness as a species, Potter shows a remarkable ability to invest the rabbits with a variety of characters, all of whom are consistent with rabbit nature. Her success with rabbits is particularly evident in this skill in characterizing them, and her ability to body forth these different characters comes from her close observation of a variety of them.

The stories are all inspired at least in part by the Uncle Remus stories of Joel Chandler Harris. As early as 1893 Potter illustrated these stories, probably choosing them because she was looking for illustrating possibilities to pursue as a career and because the stories contained a rabbit as the major actor. But the African-American stories were particularly unsuited for translation to the setting of the lush English country garden. The characters, no matter how hard Potter tried to

make them into Victorian gentlemen, resist any change from their basic natures as personified slaves and owners of the antebellum South.
The sole legacy of the Uncle Remus heritage occurs in two places. First, the fantasy of lavender, which the rabbits use as rabbit tobacco, was an idea that Potter found particularly engaging. It occurs first in her own private edition of *Peter Rabbit*, where she edited it out, later using it in characterizing old Mr. Bunny in *Benjamin Bunny*. Later still, in *Mr. Tod* old Mr. Bunny falls asleep from the drowsiness induced by his smoking and fails to guard his grandchildren adequately, setting off the complication in plot. The second legacy from Uncle Remus appears in the onomatopoeia Potter used to describe the sound that a rabbit makes when it is hopping. In *Uncle Remus* Br'er Rabbit moves "lippity-clippity, clippity-lippity."[1] In *Peter Rabbit* Peter is described as making a similar sound as he hops: "lippity—lippity. . . ."[2] Though Potter certainly knew the Harris stories, her characters, perhaps with the exception of Mr. Tod, are not modeled after Harris's. Whereas Br'er Rabbit is wily and wins by cunning, Peter and Benjamin succeed by ill-considered adventurousness and just plain luck. None of the rabbits is as motivated by vengeance as is Harris's rabbit. Though their world can be just as hard and unsympathetic as Br'er Rabbit's, the world that Potter creates for her rabbits is altogether a pleasanter, more abundant place.

The Tale of Peter Rabbit

In 1893 Potter wrote the first of many picture letters to Noel Moore, young son of her former governess and companion. The opening of the letter suggests that though she knew how to appeal to children in her writing, she really did not know how to deal with them individually: "I don't know what to write to you, so I shall tell you a story about four little rabbits."[3] She could deal with children as audience; as people, she found them somewhat problematic. The letter telling the earliest version of the Peter Rabbit story follows, written as spontaneously as most letters are, but with that late-Victorian sense of the letter as requiring considerably more attention to style than we grant to epistles today. The story has the same basic movement as the final, published form: Mother Rabbit's taboo against going into Mr. McGregor's garden, Peter's transgression, near capture, final escape, and therapeutic dosing with chamomile tea. It is a shortened version, eight duodecimo sheets including both text and illustrations, but Noel Moore considered the story good enough to have preserved the letter so that Potter could have it back and expand it when she decided to write and illustrate the book.

In 1901, when she finally found the courage both to write and then publish a book on her own, Potter asked for the letter back and began to expand the story. This version contained forty-one illustrations, including considerably expanded motivation for Peter and his escapades and a false start at the story of Benjamin Bunny, that was later eliminated to form a separate story. After sending the book to several publishers, all of whom rejected it, Potter decided to publish the book on her own. To finance the project, she used a gift of old bank stocks that her father had given her. The little book had a moderate success in the Potter family and among their acquaintances. When the first edition of five hundred was disposed of, either by sale or by gift of the author, Potter proceeded to have another edition printed, this time of two hundred and fifty copies, after making revisions to both text and illustrations.

Emboldened by the story's success in her family, she decided to submit the book one more time to the only publisher who had shown even polite interest in the project. Now that they could see a bound version of the story, Frederick Warne and Company decided to take the project, to be issued in time for the Christmas season of 1902. When the publishers reconsidered their decision, they did so with the proviso that Potter agree to color the pictures and reduce their number to thirty-two, down from the forty-one of the private edition, and later to thirty plus a frontispiece.

Though the texts of the letter, the private edition, and the final edition now commonly available are all accessible to scholars, there has been surprisingly little comment on the nature of these revisions or on the reasons for them. But the revisions are significant, for they show the evolution of Potter's style, both of writing and of illustration. They do much to explain the kind of writer and illustrator she was becoming. For the most part, the changes slow the narrative down and contribute to a greater sense of the location of the narrative in the flow of time. The revisions also clarify motivation and mold the point of view in the story as that of the small rabbit invading the human domain.

The Letter to the Private Edition. In 1893 Beatrix Potter wrote and illustrated the original version of *Peter Rabbit*. The picture letter is only eight single pages long. A comparison to the edition available today is more noteworthy for its similarity to the final printed version than for the changes Potter made. Though the letter contained only handwritten text and pen-and-ink sketches, most of the pictures are virtually the same in subject and pose. The text is arranged on the page in a way similar to the final edition. The changes are most significant in the punctuation. Frequently, in the final version Potter inserts a comma where there was no punctuation before, as in the line, "Mr. McGregor was planting out young cabbages but he jumped up & ran after Peter waving a rake & calling out 'Stop thief'!"[*sic*](*H* 14). There is no internal punctuation in the entire line as she wrote it in her letter.

In the final edition the line reads, "Mr. McGregor was on his hands and knees planting out young cabbages, but he jumped up and ran after Peter, waving a rake and calling out, 'Stop thief!'"(26). The commas merely slow down the line; perhaps they break the sentence up into smaller and more easily comprehended lines for the young reader or listener. But Potter's primary consideration would seem not to be grammar, but pacing. There are several other lines that are ended with semicolons rather than commas. Other individual sentences are broken up into two separate sentences, sometimes placing the halves on separate pages, the page turning increasing the sense of the passage of time. All of these punctuational differences underscore that the final version of *Peter Rabbit* is a longer, more substantial work than the first rough draft. The slower pacing better fits a story of more tension and more enduring significance than the short incident in the original story letter.

There are few alterations of the actual sentences between letter and first edition, an amazing situation when one considers the seven years that elapsed between the writing of the letter and Potter's decision to publish the book on her own. It also indicates the power of her intuition about what makes a good picture storybook. The lack of revision does not indicate that Potter was a less-than-conscientious writer or illustrator. Rather, it signals the soundness of her first impulses about the stories. Even a story composed as quickly and with as little effort as the letter shows almost infallible judgment about her art and her audience.

The one deletion of text from the letter underscores the carefulness with which she imagined her fantasy about animals when she came to write the book. Animals without clothing are less likely to be personified. In *Peter Rabbit* Potter strove to be consistent about the change that clothing conferred on her animals, but she also wished to be subtle about the dehumanizing nature of animal nudity. In the letter, after reporting that Peter had lost both shoes and jacket, Potter includes a half-line of description about Peter's getaway: "After losing them he ran on four legs & went faster . . ."(*H* 15). The fact that Peter is now no longer naughty boy, but has reverted to his rabbit nature, is obvious from the pictures, where in jacket he is upright and in nakedness he is four-legged. The line is a heavy-handed way for the author to make the point that the whole story, and its sequel, *Benjamin Bunny,* makes about Peter's need for his clothes to be a whole rabbit and not just an unthinking creature. Her judgment to cut the line eliminates the redundancy.

By the time Potter had decided to publish Peter's story in her own private edition, she had a sense of the picture storybook as being a more expansive genre than the picture letter. Consequently, she added a number of parts to the story that make it a story rather than a vignette or anecdote. Old Mrs. Rabbit's reason for declaring Mr. McGregor's garden off-limits is not articulated in the letter. In the first private edition the motivation is clearer: "Your Father had an accident there; he was put in a pie by Mrs. McGregor"(*H* 41). Though the picture of Mrs. McGregor and pie was deleted from the final edition, yet the line of explanation remains, to show that Peter is not simply irrationally willful in his violation of the sanction; he is also imperiled and daring. His defiant response is delayed by his mother's explanation, giving the illusion of at least a flickering of deliberation before he runs away. Once again, Potter has not only given more motivation, she has slowed down the action. Mrs. Rabbit's shopping trip is also added, thereby more clearly disposing of any parental interference and leaving the stage clear for Peter to perform, but delaying his departure for the garden until his mother leaves.

Peter's adventure in the toolshed, sitting in the watering can and risking discovery with his sneezing, is also added in this first private edition. The further adventures of Peter in trying to escape underscore his temerity and complicate the narrative, so that it is no longer a simple fable about good bunnies always obeying. The interpolation increases the tension about Peter's eventual escape, and the added pictures, showing Peter in the watering can, Mr. McGregor's hot pursuit, and Peter's eventual escape, flesh out the story and extend it. Together they explain more clearly why Peter needs dosing with chamomile at the end: not only to soothe his stomach, but also to ward off a cold, especially since his later adventures include wet feet and inadequate protection from the cold.

Potter also added in her private edition a short digression about how

Mrs. Rabbit, the widow rabbit-lady with four young offspring to care for, makes her living: by knitting and by growing and selling herbs, especially lavender, which doubles as rabbit tobacco. Again the interpolation slows down the narrative and increases tension, but this time the digression is a misleading detour. The picture and text about the old buck rabbit smoking a pipe separate the climax of Peter's return home and the denouement of his being sent to bed with only medicine for supper. This particular interpolation would seem to have been added to explain why Mrs. Rabbit is so exasperated about Peter's losing his jacket and shoes: she is a mother of limited means and cannot afford Peter's naughtiness. But her frustration with his carelessness is clear enough from the preceding line, "It was the second little jacket and pair of shoes that Peter had lost in a fortnight!" (*H* 56).

Creating sympathy for Mrs. Rabbit's poverty only increases the moralistic tone of the book and sends the reader's sympathies off in the wrong direction. After all, most readers find Peter's transgressions utterly engaging and are not prepared to shift their approbation from son to mother. Fortunately, Potter was persuaded to cut this interpolation to the beginning of the sequel to *Peter Rabbit,* where it more fittingly creates setting and, bereft of the idea of Mrs. Rabbit's poverty, develops the conception of the rabbit world as a complete and parallel one to the world of humans, with entrepreneurial cottage industries to support the economy.

Potter added a section where Peter hears Mr. McGregor whistling "Three Blind Mice," a rather ominous indication of the farmer's attitude toward stray animals. But Mr. McGregor's almost genetic aversion to small intruders is clear from the hot pursuit in which he had followed Peter, so that the incident creates a surfeit of tension; Potter wisely cut the scene from the final edition. Also in the private edition Potter added the incident where Peter arrives at the pond and sees the cat looking at its reflection in the water. The scene further develops Peter's peril and rabbitlike timidity about getting out of the garden, and further complicates the plot and accentuates the reader's anxiety about Peter's fate. But the description becomes too expansive and detracts from the adventure part of the book as a third-person limited narration. In the final Warne edition Potter shortened her description considerably.

She also added a number of phrases in the private edition to indicate the passage of time. Mrs. Rabbit delivers her injunction about going into the garden "one morning":"'Now, my dears,' said old Mrs. Rabbit one morning . . . "(*H* 40). This addition, coupled with the new beginning "Once upon a time," sets the story in some mythical past, and yet, like the beginning of the fairy tale, it renders the story eternally present, set in any time. She also altered the line in the letter that reads, "and this time he found the gate, slipped underneath and ran home safely" (*H* 16) to "He slipped underneath the gate, and was safe at last in the wood outside the garden" (*H* 55). The finality of "at last" signals to the reader that Peter's adventure is over, except for the denouement of returning home. The signal gives the reader a chance to breathe a sigh of relief. It indicates a change in the story and leads to that final wrapping up of details expected in a denouement.

The privately printed edition also added a number of pictures that the letter version did not have, as one might have expected, given the expanded text. There is also in each illustration more background than the rapid sketches the letter supplied. Giving greater background is another device Potter used to supply a kind of timelessness to the story. In the greater specificity of the garden and the wood where Peter lives, one sees a landscape that is more particularized, with colors of landscape and individual plants filling out the garden's formerly sketchy contents. One also sees a garden noteworthy for its fullness of detail and yet curiously unspecified in its setting. Most gardens and most woods in Western countries look like this, and any place where gardens like these exist, one is likely to find both gardeners and rabbits. Neither Peter nor his family nor Mr. McGregor are such peculiar types that they belong only to one time or one place. Thus, in giving the illustrations more detail, Potter managed to give less time- and place-bound specificity. Therein lies at least part of the story's perennial appeal to children in many cultures. The numerous foreign-language translations of the book attest to Peter's appeal in many different places over the last eighty-odd years.

The First Private Edition to the Second Private Edition. When Potter reprinted her private edition, she edited the text again, though only in small details. Yet these revisions are also significant, for they demonstrate her tireless quest for just the right angle in illustration, just the right word and cadence. For example, when she went to the second private edition, she reexamined the incident where Peter asks a mouse to help him find his way out of the garden. But the mouse is only an animal and not personified the way Peter is, so of course she does not speak to him. In the first edition Potter narrates, "She shook her head at him" (*H* 52). In the second edition Potter inserts a single word: "only": "She only shook her head at him."[4] The word "only" underscores the fact that the mouse either cannot or will not speak to Peter. Her aid is limited, and Peter is the only one concerned with his problem. He is an only rabbit, alone in the world, with no one to help him. The results of the single word are multiple: meaning is clarified and enhanced, and the little rabbit acquires sympathy for his plight where formerly there was only admiration for his bold-faced mischievousness.

Potter further clarifies meaning elsewhere. The narrative in the first edition reads, "He went towards the tool-shed again, but suddenly there was a most peculiar noise—scr-r-ritch, scratch, scratch, scritch" (*H* 53). The onomatopoeia makes the noise even more peculiar, for Potter has made up the noise. Its transliteration into speech is not a familiar noise that all English speakers recognize, the way that they know ding-dong or bow-wow. The story is, after all, directed toward a very young audience, perhaps even a preliterate one whose competence with the language is somewhat limited and who cannot be expected to guess with any accuracy what the onomatopoeia means.

In the second edition Potter rectifies the ambiguity: "He went back towards the tool-shed, but suddenly, quite close to him, he heard the noise of a hoe—scr-r-ritch scratch, scratch, scratch."[5] This time, the onomatopoeia is identified for the young reader, and its import made all the more dramatic because its source is "quite close to him." This time, too, the sound is not one of repetition or reversal, the way that "scr-r-ritch, scratch, scratch, scritch" is. This time, "scr-r-ritch scratch, scratch, scratch," with the initial comma eliminated and the final "scritch" changed to a "scratch," sounds more like an activity just begun and continuing, rather than repeating itself by going back and forth. In other words, not only is the onomatopoeia clearer, it is also more accurate.

The Second Private Edition to the Warne Edition.   Even as Potter submitted her book to the scrutiny of the Warne editors, she continued to revise it. She deleted the following sentences from the second edition when editing it for Warne: "There surely never *was* such a garden for cabbages! Hundreds and hundreds of them; and Peter was not tall enough to see over them, and felt too sick to eat them. It was just like a very bad dream!" (*H* 52) These lines add little to the pictures that already show Peter as quite small compared to the garden's contents. His illness from overeating is made clear earlier, and the "bad dream" quality of his experience should be obvious from the rest of the narration. Potter also altered the line, "In the middle of the garden he came to the pond" (*H* 53) to "Presently, he came to the pond" (46). Peter is clearly in the midst of the garden once he goes over the wall. The pond's location in the middle is quite immaterial and perhaps even unknowable to the short and therefore hardly omniscient rabbit. "Presently" is the word that Potter uses elsewhere to indicate the passage of time, perhaps rather vaguely but accurately enough for the situation here. Once again she altered her hoeing onomatopoeia back to its original "scr-r-ritch, scratch, scratch, scritch"[6] to underscore the repetitious motion.

In a move for economy of language Potter deleted the phrase "In consequence of having eaten too much in Mr. McGregor's garden" from the sentence which begins, "I am sorry to say Peter was not very well during the evening" (*H* 58). His overindulgence has already been noted, as has his plunge bath in the watering can and his fright. Any and all of these could have resulted in his ill health. By deletion, this time Potter has added to the meaning, rather than diminishing by such clarification.

She was also tireless in her revision of illustrations for the story. The original cover illustration for the Warne edition was certainly satisfactory, but she decided to redraw Peter, this time showing more action in his lower torso, and thereby indicating more speed in his scampering. She also changed the expression in his eye, showing less terror and more mischievous defiance and innocent impetus toward fun and adventure. These are all emotions more consistent with the story and less indicative of a moral. She also tried a number of times to improve her illustration of Mrs. McGregor and the pie containing Peter's father; but her skill in illustrating humans was never equal to her portrayal of animals. Even when she used herself as a model for Mrs. McGregor, neither she nor her publishers was satisfied, and together they decided to eliminate the picture altogether.

After the fourth edition Potter went on to other books and the text remained unchanged from then on. However, she took an active interest in the numerous translations of *Peter Rabbit* into foreign languages. As to the French version as first shown to her, she said, "That French is choke [*sic*] full of mistakes both in spelling and grammar. I dare say it is the English type-writer's slip-shod reading of the M.S.S." The final version was more to her taste: "It is just right—colloquial without being slangy."[7] Her businesswoman's sense of lucrative foreign markets stayed with her as she wrote later books. For instance, she was always careful to leave out any printing on street signs in the pictures, to avoid the difficulties posed by idiomatic translation of the words.

Between *Peter Rabbit* and *Benjamin Bunny* Potter wrote and published *Squirrel Nutkin* and *The Tailor of Gloucester,* but the reading public, as pleased as it was with her squirrel and mouse stories, demanded more bunnies. Benjamin Bunny had already been fabricated as a false start in the *Peter Rabbit* story, and the deleted material was just waiting for the rest of Benjamin's story to be told.

Popularity. The popularity of *Peter Rabbit* has much to do with its timeless quality. The pictures and themes seem to be those of some past age, perhaps a pretechnological period, but no particular century. The enmity between humans and wild animals is a situation that has endured since the human race decided to take up farming. The outwitting of the large and powerful by the small and cunning is as old as David and Goliath, and is an archetype dear to the heart of any one who perceives that the world has victimized him. Children have always wanted to do what their parents have told them not to since Adam and Eve disobeyed. And parents have taken their misguided offspring back into the family ever since Genesis, when God gave His creatures the rest of His creation to live in. The archetypes upon which Potter modeled the exquisitely small story of the wayward rabbit are indeed large and timeless.

The illustrations also underscore the unspecified past intruding on the present that the text portrays. Mrs. Rabbit going forth on her shopping trip through the woods looks suspiciously like Little Red Riding-Hood, except that she has an umbrella. But the umbrella does not violate the sense of history in the picture as much as it underscores the sense of motherly anxiety. The lady rabbit is just cautious about the unexpected. Her anxiety about the possible excess of rain or sun from which the umbrella will protect her is a further extension of her anxiety about her children. The rabbit children wear out-of-style short cloaks or jackets of an unspecified past, but Peter wears blue, whereas his sisters wear deep pink, a sex differentiation by color handed down from the ancient Romans. And Peter's shoes are clogs or pumps, but no so fashionably portrayed that they are identifiable as anything but antique.

When Potter colored the pen-and-ink drawings of her private edition for Frederick Warne's edition, she had to do something about framing the backgrounds. Instead of having the pictures end at the edge of the paper, she chose to vignette them, that is, to enclose the colored pictures in an oval space of white, similar to an old-fashioned cameo or portrait photograph. This technique, too, lends to the pictures a sense of antiquity, of tastes formerly popular but no longer so. And the colors she used, almost translucent pastels, with a predominance of natural tones of green and brown, communicate a sense of fading from original brilliance and yet endurance in the dominance of the colors from nature in the rabbits and garden foliage.

Perhaps the major reason that *The Tale of Peter Rabbit* endures is the sense of the world that Potter created as ongoing, as permanent, uninterrupted by historical events or the intervening years. Rabbit and gardener continue to go about their business with no regard for the reader's visual intrusion into their fictionalized world. Any eye contact between reader and character is fleeting and of no purpose. Mr. McGregor returns to his gardening when he fails to catch Peter. Peter returns home and is nursed back to health, to raid and raze another day. The ending may be a closed one, but neither Peter's life nor Mr. McGregor's garden is irrevocably altered by the adventure, and modern technology and urbanization seem to have little influence on the relationships between gardeners and rabbits. Though publishing practices and popular tastes in children's literature change, yet the story of the rabbit and the farmer do not, except in bowdlerized and cheap reissues. The text and illustrations are reliable and enduring, and if the Easter Bunny is also named Peter, it is because his namesake is as perennial as he is.

The Tale of Benjamin Bunny

By 1903 it was clear to the Warne company that Beatrix Potter's miniature library was a great money-maker. Therefore, it is not surprising to find that Warne was now asking the author for more books, rather than waiting for her to publish them on her own first. By 1903 Beatrix Potter had published three books with the company: *Peter Rabbit, The Tailor of Gloucester,* and *Squirrel Nutkin.* Most of the well-developed ideas she had on hand had been made into books. So, when Warne requested another book, to be published simultaneously with *The Tale of Two Bad Mice,* Potter turned to a part of the *Peter Rabbit* story that had been eliminated from her own privately printed edition because it was not really relevant. Benjamin Bunny had been mentioned by name in the early edition of *Peter Rabbit,* but he was not a character in the story. He had simply been mentioned in a casual aside.

A picture of Old Mr. Benjamin Bunny, little Benjamin's father, was included in the early edition, but he too has no active part in the story. Here were two characters just waiting to be created and equipped with personalities. Potter turned to them for her next story.

She wrote to Norman Warne that she thought *The Tailor of Gloucester* and *Squirrel Nutkin* were stories of considerably more plot complication than *Peter Rabbit*. She therefore suggested that a simpler story might be in order to satisfy her younger audience. As Peter's cousin, Benjamin seemed a likely character for a story similar to Peter's. In fact, *Benjamin Bunny* is a sequel to *Peter Rabbit*, which literally goes over the same ground as the first story.

Benjamin Bunny goes to visit his cousin one day not long after Peter's initial adventure, and finds Peter without clothes, wrapped in a thin cotton handkerchief, huddling in the corner of the rabbit hole. When he finds out that Peter's clothes are still in Mr. McGregor's garden, Benjamin suggests that they retrieve the jacket and shoes on a return visit. Though Peter is apprehensive, his mother's voice in the background calling for more chamomile to make medicine for him spurs him on to follow Benjamin.

Benjamin, who is a habitual raider of the garden, shows Peter how to get over the wall without damaging his clothes, by climbing up a pear tree. The two manage to retrieve the clothes from Mr McGregor's scarecrow and even to collect a bunch of onions as a peace offering to Mrs. Rabbit. But their safe retreat to the rabbit hole is imperiled by Mr. McGregor's cat, who traps the cousins under a basket. The fearless Old Mr. Benjamin Bunny has been out looking for the two young rabbits and drives the cat off with his switch, which he then turns on Peter and Benjamin to punish them. When they arrive home, the two are penitent but readily forgiven, for the gift of onions both satisfies and distracts Mrs. Bunny. Certainly she is glad that Peter has his clothes back.

Potter was persuaded by Norman Warne to cut her interpolation about Mrs. Rabbit's profession to the beginning of the sequel to *Benjamin Bunny*, where it more fittingly creates setting. Bereft of the idea of Mrs. Rabbit's poverty, the passage develops the conception of the rabbit world as a complete unto itself. Thus, Potter's rabbit world becomes larger and more convincing, a universe clearly parallel to the human world.

In this world rabbits have extended families, as humans do; in fact, the rabbit boys pair off the same way that human boys do. Benjamin is the adventurous and knowledgeable cousin, Peter's doppelgänger in effect. Graham Green calls Peter and Benjamin "epic personalities" who are "paired" like Quixote and Sancho, or Pickwick and Weller.[8] In this duo it is Benjamin and not Peter who notices at the beginning of the story that Mr. and Mrs. McGregor are going out in their gig. He infers that they will be gone for the whole day, since he notices that Mrs. McGregor is wearing her best bonnet. These are the clues he uses to convince the unwilling Peter to go along with him on a visit to the garden. Peter took no such precautions on his solo adventure. When Benjamin sees Peter huddling in the corner of the rabbit hole, wearing only a red bandana handkerchief, he uses the pretext of retrieving the lost shoes and jacket to gain some glory and adventure while doing what he wanted to do in the first place. Like Huck Finn and Tom Sawyer, Benjamin looks for the glamorous adventure, while Peter's less-than-willing participation results from his desire to be a loyal follower.

Though Peter managed to get into the garden the first time without Benjamin's help, it is Benjamin who knows that "it spoils people's clothes to squeeze under a gate; the proper way to get in, is to climb down a pear tree." Benjamin manages this unrabbitlike feat with ease, but Peter, his inept sidekick, "fell down head first."[9] It is Benjamin, who, like Tom Sawyer, directs the exploit: "Little Benjamin said that the first thing to be done was to get back Peter's clothes, in order that they might be able to use the pocket-handkerchief" (29). And it is Benjamin who knows that the handkerchief can be used to placate Peter's overanxious mother: "Then he suggested that they should fill the pocket-handkerchief with onions, as a little present for his Aunt" (30).

Even though "Peter did not seem to be enjoying himself; he kept hearing noises" (30), Benjamin proceeds to revel in the bounty of the garden, explaining that "he was in the habit of coming to the garden with his father to get lettuces for their Sunday dinner" (33), and implying that Peter is worrying for nothing. When it is time to leave and the onions prevent them from taking the pear tree route again, Benjamin "led the way boldly towards the other end of the garden" (37), with no regard for the peril that Peter encountered on the same route during his last trip. But Peter is aware of the danger, as signaled by his twice dropping the handkerchief and its contents, without any other explanation from Potter.

Peter and Benjamin do not escape without trouble, since they are trapped by a cat, then rescued and punished by Benjamin's father. But Benjamin's story does not end with sick rabbits and chamomile, like Peter's: "When Peter got home, his mother forgave him, because she was so glad to see that he had found his shoes and coat." The peace offering does not go unnoticed either: "Cotton-tail and Peter folded up the pocket-handkerchief, and old Mrs. Rabbit strung up the onions and hung them from the kitchen ceiling, with the bunches of herbs and the rabbit-tobacco" (59). So the adventure may be considered to have been a success, even though Peter and Benjamin are marched out of the garden in tears, followed by Old Mr. Benjamin Bunny and his ominous switch.

Evidently, the Warne company did not like the ending as Potter had originally written it, for she commented in a letter to them that she would like to change their suggestion "they lived happily etc.," for, as she said in the letter, "In the first place it is inexact, also rather a trite ending." She suggested the last paragraph as it stands now, with the comment, "If the above is too long—leave out C. Tail and Peter etc. and say 'and she strung up' etc. I would like the book to end with the word 'rabbit-tobacco', it is a rather fine word."[10] Here is evidence of a writer who knows the truth of what she writes. She will not gloss over the fact that the two rabbits have been rather summarily punished, even if at the end their exploits are forgiven, since it is the end rather than the means that is most noteworthy. Potter also put particular emphasis on her beginnings and endings, and it is rare to see her reverting to the trite or conventional at these key points in her books.

In her revisions Potter also shows her flair for what she called the "fine word," and her willingness to fight for the right word in the right place. Earlier in her correspondence about *Benjamin Bunny* she suggested using the word "conversed" in the book because, as she said, "children like a fine word occasionally."[11] Just because her audience was young, she would not accede to a simplified vocabulary. She understood that children recognize more vocabulary than they are able to use, and that if the word is unfamiliar, its meaning may be surmised and learned from a clearly described context. She strove toward this clear context in her revisions. In the same letter that she suggested the word "conversed," she also suggested using "winked" instead of "looked" in the sentence "The mice sat on their doorsteps cracking cherry-stones, they winked at Peter Rabbit and Little Benjamin Bunny" (37). Winking much more clearly describes the kind of gaze that mice are capable of, than does the more generic "looking." She also complained of the editing of "underneath" in the sentence "I cannot draw you a picture of Peter and Benjamin underneath the basket, because it was quite dark, and because the smell of the onions was fearful . . ." (46). The editors had changed "underneath" to "under." Potter objected: "I think that would a little alter the sense? by under*neath* I mean an inside view."[12] In other words, the impossible picture should conjure up the sight not only of the two rabbits, but also of the basket that imprisons and menaces them.

She kept working on the text right up to the time of publication, when she altered these two one-sentence paragraphs:

> When Mr. McGregor returned only 10 minutes later, he observed several things that perplexed him.
> Especially he could not comprehend how the cat had shut herself into the green-house and locked the door upon the outside.

She first revised the text to read:

> When Mr. McGregor returned about half an hour later, he observed several things which perplexed him; also he could not understand how the cat could have managed to shut herself up inside the green-house locking the door upon the *outside.*
> It looked as though some person had been walking all over the garden in a pair of clogs—only the footmarks were so curiously little.[13]

Here is the text as it finally reads:

> When Mr. McGregor returned about half an hour later, he observed several things which perplexed him.
> It looked as though some person had been walking all over the garden in a pair of clogs—only the foot-marks were too ridiculously little!
> Also he could not understand how the cat could have managed to shut herself up *inside* the green-house, locking the door upon the *outside.* (56)

The first version does not follow the logic of the sentence or the situation. Mr. McGregor is confused, but one of the many things that confuses him is the cat's mislocation. It is not in addition to the many other confusing aspects of the situation. The intermediate revision confuses the time sequence in which Mr. McGregor discovers his perplexities. He sees the garden and the footprints first and then discovers the cat in the shed. The revision also makes the footprints merely "curious" instead of the more preposterous "ridiculous" which their size truly makes them. The final version straightens out both time sequence and reaction to the variety of confusing occurrences facing Mr. McGregor.

Though Potter originally designed the book for younger readers, yet it is still full of her understated humor. For instance, when Benjamin particularly avoids his aunt on his visit, a naive reader may miss the joke that he avoids her so that she will not stop him from going back into the garden, which she had expressly forbidden Peter to do. Peter's conclusion that "he might feel better if he went for a walk" (21) when he hears the call for more chamomile is persiflage, to cover up his avoidance of the bitter medicine. His constant dropping and falling throughout the adventure seem unmotivated and purely accidental as the text is narrated. But inference makes clear his lack of nerve and daring, and the anxiety that causes his accidents. The book is as rich an experience for the sophisticated reader as it is for the young child, and the various levels of meaning and quiet jokes that may not be available to the child keep the book from becoming too simple and uninteresting for the older reader.

When Potter first turned to write *Benjamin Bunny,* she frankly admitted to her publisher that she had run out of ideas for drawings and that she would have to spend some time collecting more sketches of bunnies and gardens. This collecting process went on while she and her family were on summer holiday at Fawe Park, Keswick. There she found the proper kinds of lettuces—Linder reports that they are the variety called "Sutton's Perfection"[14]—and the proper poses for her rabbits. The cat that terrorizes Peter and Benjamin while they are under the basket is a tiger who looks remarkably like Simpkin, the cat in *The Tailor of Gloucester.* There were a few pictures that Potter labored over. She was apparently in a hurry when she drew the picture of Old Mr. Bunny attacking the cat, and the first drawing was not satisfactory to the publisher. In her home, which is now a museum, the original drawing is on display, showing the rabbit with his neck at a curious, unnatural angle, as he jumps down on top of the cat. Potter redrew the picture, and though the rabbit's neck still has a peculiar bend to it, the angle is not nearly as odd as in the original drawing. Because she lifts the rabbit's head up in the redrawing, his eye is more visible from a more direct angle, and the reader has a moment of eye-contact, of flickering recognition, when first viewing the picture.

She also redrew the picture of the rabbit cousins on top of the wall, looking into the garden before they enter it. In her revision she made the rabbits larger, and their ears more flared to their sides. The larger rabbits standing on the wall frame the vista of the garden more emphatically, partly because they are larger and partly because they are drawn in darker shades. The clearer frame makes the watery pastels of the garden seem more faint and creates the illusion of greater depth in the picture. The garden seems larger and the distance to the other side much greater in the revision. The change in the position of the rabbits' ears, with them twisting out more and pointing more directly upward, gives motion to their bodies and makes them seem more alert, more anxious and eager. By inference, Peter's ears are at anxious attention to hear the many frightening sounds that plague him on this adventure. Benjamin's are on full alert because of his anticipatory eagerness about the adventure. The revisions are altogether more satisfactory than the first versions, and one suspects Potter of false humility when she wrote to her publisher about them, "The worst of copying drawings a second time is that I get so confused I don't know whether they are worse or better. Please don't hesitate to send them back if they are still wrong. . . ."15

The care that Potter took in the drawings is obvious elsewhere. The robin whose presence is so ubiquitous in *Peter Rabbit* again appears, again as an unmentioned observer, in the picture of Benjamin and Peter wandering "amongst flowerpots, and frames and tubs" (41). Flopsy, Mopsy, and Cottontail are again presented as rabbits of limited rabbit minds, for they all huddle together close to their mother and do not wear clothes. Potter deliberately chose a red handkerchief for Peter to wear, so that the color would stand as a bright contrast to his blue jacket and Benjamin's brown one. The clog prints that so puzzle Mr. McGregor are made by footgear clearly in evidence as Peter rescues his own from the scarecrow, and they show Potter's careful attention to detail.

Finally, the wild red campion growing as overlooked weeds in Mr. McGregor's garden are legion in the Lake District where Potter spent her time sketching in the summer of 1903. The book's dedication "For the children of Sawrey from Old Mr. Bunny" (7) and the wealth of detail about Lake District vegetable gardens in the pictures show Potter's increasing attraction to Sawrey and its environs. Whereas Peter Rabbit's garden is a Scottish one, drawn while the Potters were on holiday in Perthshire, Potter moved the whole Rabbit-Bunny clan to the Lakes and kept them there in the sequel, *Mr. Tod.*

The Flopsy Bunnies

By 1909 it was clear, both to Potter and her publishers, that though her other works were popular enough with her public, it was the Rabbit-Bunny books that had made and continued to maintain her reputation. During a vacation in Wales with her aunt and uncle in 1909, Potter had sketched their elegantly manicured walled garden, and when she returned home, she had decided to move Peter and Benjamin and their families to Wales for another Peter Rabbit sequel, *The Tale of the Flopsy Bunnies*.

In this story Peter and Benjamin are grown rabbits, and Benjamin Bunny has married his cousin Flopsy; hence the family name, Flopsy Bunnies. They have a young family of their own, but no means to support themselves. Whereas Mrs. Rabbit had established herself in *Benjamin Bunny* as a rabbit of enterprise, in *The Flopsy Bunnies* she and Peter have gone into business for themselves. The sign over their business, included in Potter's original frontispiece, reads "Peter Rabbit & Mother—Florists—Gardens neatly razed. Borders devastated by the night or year."[16] So it is Peter, the businessman, to whom the Flopsy Bunnies turn when they do not have enough to eat. On those occasions when even Peter cannot supply them, they again return to Mr. Mc-Gregor's garden, this time to the rubbish heap, where on this particular day Mr. McGregor has discarded some overgrown lettuces, along with the rotten vegetables and lawn clippings that the bunnies usually expect to find there. Owing to their "improvident and cheerful" natures[17] and to the "soporific" (9) influence of lettuces, all the baby bunnies fall asleep on top of the rubbish heap, while their father is temporarily distracted by a conversation with a neighboring wood mouse. Mr. McGregor comes upon them by surprise and, discovering the baby bunnies, puts them in a sack and ties it closed. Benjamin, the father rabbit, is helpless to do anything. When Flopsy, who had stayed home but owing to their long absence goes looking for them all, arrives, all that the worried father can do is explain. The wood mouse saves the young ones by gnawing a hole in the sack to let the babies out, and the parents stuff the sack with six assorted objects from the rubbish heap to fool the farmer. Then all the animals retreat to the bushes to watch the farmer's reaction.

At first, he does not notice the substitution, but when he brings the sack home to his wife, claiming that there are six little rabbits inside, Mrs. McGregor feels the shapes and protests that they are too hard to be young and will hardly be worth eating. She claims their skins for herself, though Mr. McGregor protests and reclaims them for sale so that he can buy tobacco. The scene is set for marital discord, and when Mrs. McGregor reaches inside and finds the rotten vegetable substitutes, she blames her husband for tricking her. Though it is unclear who throws it, one rotten vegetable comes flying through the window where the Flopsy bunnies are watching. The rabbit family decides to retreat and let the couple work out their problems by themselves. The book ends with a Christmas gift to the mouse of some rabbit wool for her own use.

The story is once again one of the rabbits intruding upon the humans' domain and by their own imprudence bringing down upon themselves the threats of death and destruction. Peter Rabbit seems to have chosen a more prudent way of handling his intrusions by tending his own private cabbage patch. But even here one suspects that Peter is more of a prudent harvester of human crops than he is an actual gardener. The rubbish heap is just outside the garden wall, but the wall itself is a human construct, as is the rubbish heap, and the rabbits trespass at their own peril. It would seem that the wall is more a mark of human domination than a definite territorial boundary.

Once again, the story is also about human interaction with animals, and, once again, Potter had to deal with the problem of drawing humans. This time she solved many of the problems of portraying Mr. McGregor by showing mostly his hands or his feet, as the rabbits might have seen them, but rarely his whole body. Though the various appendages are still clumsy, especially as compared to the exquisite portraits of the bunnies, yet the clumsiness of the human portraits is not as obvious because the arms and feet are in isolation. The one full-length portrait of Mr. McGregor shows him from a rear view, again minimizing the lack of skill with which Potter drew humans and eliminating the difficulties of drawing his face. The bunnies, on the other hand, are drawn with Potter's usual precision and ability to show, from a slight angle in the lift of the tail or a small twist in the attitude of the ear, the various human attributes with which she wished to endow the rabbits. The baby bunnies are not individualized, as befits their lack of separate names and their general patronym, the Flopsy Bunnies. Peter Rabbit still wears his blue jacket and Benjamin a red one for contrast. Peter's mother wears a pink-striped dress, of different fabric, but of the same style as her dress when she walked through the woods on her shopping trip in *Peter Rabbit*. Flopsy is the one rabbit who seems incompletely clothed, for she wears a large blue apron that covers her front, but leaves her tail showing in the back. Though the apron makes her seem motherly enough, her "improvident and cheerful" nature seems evident in that incomplete attire. She does not worry enough to keep herself adequately dressed by human standards. Still, her tail is a useful device by which to show emotion, as noted before, and perhaps this is why Flopsy is not as completely clothed as her mother. In the picture of Flopsy cautiously walking up the lawn to the house it is only by the tail and the position of her ears that Potter manages to evoke the panic and apprehension that the small rabbit feels in the wide open space belonging to the humans.

Unlike the previous Peter Rabbit–Benjamin Bunny books, the garden here receives more attention in the pictures than it did in previous rabbit books. Perhaps this is because Potter knew that her visit to her relatives in Gwaynynog was meant as a sketching expedition for backgrounds for the book. The garden here is a very different one from that in *Peter Rabbit* and *Benjamin Bunny*, with many more flowers, archways, and formal beds than in the kitchen garden of the former books. And the long vistas of the flower garden that are so prominently featured dwarf the rabbits while emphasizing the floral beauty of the flower beds. Though the book is simple in plot and designed to capture the attention of the young reader, one suspects that Potter was more involved in the locale of the book than in the characters themselves. In any case, her dedication of *The Flopsy Bunnies* "For All Little Friends of Mr. McGregor & Peter & Benjamin" (7) indicates that she knew her audience for the book was nearly guaranteed. The dedication also suggests that she assumed the creation of character in the former books and the carryover of character into the present one. Elsewhere she had complained that the rabbit characters had become "wearisome,"[18] and the brevity with which she dealt with them suggests that this was her attitude toward this book.

As elsewhere, Potter put particular emphasis on the openings and closings of *The Flopsy Bunnies,* where the opening also shows her flair for the elevated diction seen in her former books: "It is said that the effect of eating too much lettuce is 'soporific.'" Though the word "soporific" is certainly not a common one in the young child's vocabulary, Potter is perfectly aware of her audience's limitations, for in the next line she defines the word by putting it in context: "*I* have never felt sleepy after eating lettuces; but then *I* am not a rabbit" (9). In that single line she defines not only the meaning of the word, but also the subject of the story: rabbits. Though Potter is here intruding herself into the narrative, the line does not draw attention to herself, but rather gives the book a conversational tone, a sense of the story actually being told aloud by a narrator. And because she shifts the focus immediately back to the rabbits, there is no danger of Beatrix Potter becoming a character in the book; elsewhere she is invisible.

Potter also uses fine language in the initial description of the bunny family: "They had a large family, and they were very improvident and cheerful" (10). Though the text does not immediately clarify the meaning of improvident, their cheerfulness is obvious from the family romp in the rabbit hole portrayed on the next page. Their improvidence is suggested on the following two pages of text, describing Benjamin's borrowing of cabbages from Peter, and the bunnies' occasional need to resort to Mr. McGregor's rubbish heap. Because the rubbish heap, like the gardener, is a permanent fixture in the universe that Peter and Benjamin inhabit, the threat of starvation in the phrase "As there was not always quite enough to eat" (13) is mitigated. Benjamin may not always be able to provide for his family by himself, but he does make sure that he gets food for them either from Peter or from Mr McGregor. Food is available, but it is not always Benjamin's by right. What he lacks in prudence he makes up for in cheer; thus the obscure vocabulary is defined by the course of the action. The lack of an immediate definition carries the narrative forward to satisfy the reader's curiosity about what the word may mean.

Though Mr. McGregor is only a shadowy, awkward, although still menacing presence in the pictures, for the first time he is given language, which also serves to define him. He counts the number of baby bunnies in what is presumably a Scottish accent, calling then "six leetle fat rabbits" (49). His argument with his wife about buying "baccy" (50) and her claim that her husband has tricked her and "done it a purpose" (53) shows Potter's careful attention to dialogue and dialect as methods of defining characters—in this case, of contrasting their manner of speaking with her own in narrating the story.

On the whole, the story carries on in the *Peter Rabbit* mode for the young child. Mr. McGregor does not deliberately aim to hurt the bunnies. They just happen to put themselves in the way of danger. Their rescue comes by animal ingenuity, and all the characters live to worry each other another day.

The Tale of Mr. Tod

Beatrix Potter returned one last time to the Rabbit-Bunny family for inspiration when she wrote *The Tale of Mr. Tod* in 1912. Her fatigue with writing, with coming up with what she called "'fresh' short stories,"[19] with writing about the same kinds of characters book after book, is obvious from the first line: "I have made many books about well-behaved people. Now, for a change, I am going to make a story about two disagreeable people, called Tommy Brock and Mr. Tod."[20] She was ready for a change, at least partly because she thought her editors too cautious and too concerned about offending the public. She was capable of much more complex plots and characters and wanted to give full reign to her capabilities.

The changes from Potter's earlier books are many: there are far fewer colored pictures and many more pen-and-ink sketches, of half a page or less, scattered throughout the book, with nearly one for every page. Potter complained that her eyes were no longer good enough for the careful work that colored paintings required, but even in later life she did not lose her ability to sketch. The book is also not a short one, at least not as short as *Peter Rabbit* or even *The Tailor of Gloucester*. Even when she was most reluctant to comply with her publisher's requests for more books, she still composed stories for herself, even though she did not publish them. Her willingness to work extensively with language is particularly evident here. The story is almost a novella, at least compared to the considerably more compact tales composed for younger children earlier in her career.

Because her publishers sensed that this was a different kind of Beatrix Potter story, they decided to publish it, with *Pigling Bland* in 1913, in the same sized format as the other Potter books, but with a slightly more decorative binding. The change in binding was made at least partially to accommodate the longer length and therefore the necessity for a wider spine. Though the two books were published as part of what was then called "The Peter Rabbit Books, Series II, New Style,"[21] both are now included as part of the Potter nursery collection and are bound in the same green covers as the other books in the series.

The story concerns the two villains, the enmity between them, and the complication of Tommy Brock's theft of Benjamin Bunny's new family of baby rabbits. As badgers do, Tommy Brock is perpetually invading the abandoned residences of the fox, Mr. Tod. Though Mr. Tod has half a dozen homes in various places throughout the woods around Beatrix Potter's home in Sawrey, he does from time to time change residences and return to formerly abandoned homes. When he does, he finds the badger's invasions an abomination and unspeakable contamination, both from his filthy habits and from his noxious odor. In this story Mr. Tod finds Tommy Brock still residing in one of his homes. He designs to play a trick on the badger while he is sleeping in the fox's bed so that the badger will never return. The badger out-smarts the fox and escapes to invade another day, in the process totally destroying the fox's fastidiously clean and arranged kitchen and bed. But he does not manage to make a meal of the baby rabbits, whom he steals from under the less-than-vigilant care of their paternal grand-father, old Mr. Benjamin Bouncer. Peter Rabbit and Benjamin Bunny rescue the baby rabbits from their culinary fate while Tommy Brock and Mr. Tod are carrying on their mutual revenge, and return the family safe and sound. So the rivalry between predators and prey con-tinues, as well as that between the two mortal enemies, at story's end.

Potter's desire for a change is evident from the opening paragraph. Her exasperation with the good behavior of her earlier characters is even more evident in the manuscript's opening lines: "I am quite tired of making goody goody books about nice people."[22] A version of Mr. Tod had previously appeared in *Jemima Puddle-Duck* as the suave gentle-man with the red whiskers, but the story is really not about him, but about the gullible duck. In *Mr. Tod* Potter gave herself the opportunity to tell the story of the truly evil and malevolent characters. Her incor-poration of Peter Rabbit and Benjamin and Flopsy Bunny not only insured the book's popularity with the reading and book-buying pub-lic, it also provided a foil to the guile and manipulation of the two main characters, Tommy Brock and Mr. Tod. As the rabbits are inno-cent and well-intentioned, so the two villains are irredeemable cads.

The story begins on an ominous note: the opening descriptions of the fox and the badger define them as nemeses of rabbits, for the rab-bits in the forest cannot stand the fox's smell, which they can detect "half a mile off" (7). As to the badger's eating rabbit pie, a reminis-cence of the fate of Peter Rabbit's father at Mrs. McGregor's hands, Potter seems to excuse the behavior because the rabbits were "only very little young ones occasionally, when other food was really scarce" (10). But the excuse is really no excuse, for the fact remains that baby rabbits are imperiled by badgers. Tommy Brock is a friend of old Mr. Bouncer, presuming alliance based on mutual dislike of Mr. Tod. Since the friendship between the two is an uneasy one, the reader's sympathies do not excuse Tommy Brock for preying on the young rabbits, especially since he is, as Mr. Bouncer notices, a particularly fat animal, who never really faces a scarcity of food.

The litter in Mr. Tod's home on Bull Banks Hollow, now occupied by Tommy Brock, is even more forbidding: "There were many unpleasant things lying about, that had much better have been buried; rabbit bones and skulls, and chickens' legs and other horrors. It was a shocking place . . ." (39). The destruction, accompanied by the falling darkness on the scene, underscore that this is truly a scene of horror, with none of the bloodthirsty carnivorousness held back. The baby bunnies are in mortal danger, as are the adult Peter and Benjamin, who may suffer the same fate if caught by either fox or badger.

The peril of the baby rabbits is further complicated by their grandfather's attitude toward them while he is babysitting: he does not think about them as they sleep in a burrow separated from the main rabbit hole. So when the badger stops by for a visit, the grandfather rabbit does not think about the danger the badger implies for his grandchildren. He simply chats with the badger about subjects of mutual interest, such as Mr. Tod and the local otters, and smokes the rabbit tobacco he so conspicuously consumed in *Benjamin Bunny.*

Consistent with his role as hospitable and cordial host, the elder Bunny invites Tommy Brock into the rabbit hole and offers him food and drink, including cowslip wine, which, combined with the smoke from Tommy's cabbage-leaf tobacco, puts the inattentive babysitter right to sleep. The welcoming of badger into the house, even though he is carrying a bunch of mole traps and makes jokes about turning vegetarian, which he clearly is not, underscores the naiveté of the senior rabbit and the way in which he unwittingly invites the sacrifice of the babies. The grandfather rabbit seems unable to recognize his own mortal enemies, nor the irony of Tommy Brock's presence and conversation in light of his own situation. His lack of judgment is consistent with Potter's description of him as being "stricken in years" (11), and Peter Rabbit's assessment that "My Uncle Bouncer has displayed a lamentable want of discretion for his years" (27). This is a rabbit in sad decline from his former robust vanquishing of the cat in *Benjamin Bunny.*

It is up to Peter and Benjamin to rescue the young bunnies, and they do so in a way that defines their adult characters as consistent with their youthful personalities in the earlier books. Benjamin is full of anxiety and anxious worry; he is on the verge of panic and not very helpful in planning what to do about the rescue. He is the cousin full of emotion. Peter, on the other hand, is both more cautious and more practical. His business sense, which is evident in his commercial enterprise with his mother in *The Flopsy Bunnies* and in his ability to sense real danger where Benjamin perceives only opportunities for reckless abandon in *Benjamin Bunny,* comes to the fore in his rescue plan. He assesses clues as to the whereabouts and present circumstances of the babies; he urges Benjamin on when the crucial moment comes to go into the fox's house and steal back the baby bunnies; he is altogether more thoughtful in his approach to the situation. As he says about the predicament, "Let me use my mind, Cousin Benjamin" (24). On the other hand, he is not so levelheaded that he never loses his rational judgment. When the two rabbits hear the fox coming back to his house, they both run back into the tunnel they have been digging under the fox's kitchen, into a situation in which they are trapped and from which they cannot escape. They are not so relentlessly human that they lose their timid, thoughtless, rabbit natures. It is luck, and not Peter's foresight and planning, that eventually effects the rescue.

The story has a number of inconsistencies from a naturalist's point of view. For example, foxes and badgers are not necessarily mutual enemies in nature, and though badgers do occasionally eat baby bunnies, they do not do so from any particular predisposition to young rabbit, but rather from a habit of omnivorousness.[23] Badgers do not typically take over the homes of foxes, who themselves have a rather overpowering scent, and they are not typically dirty. But the discrepancies are not major ones and are designed to create individual characters rather than summon up the archetypical fox and badger.

The story does have archetypical sources, however. Potter herself, in a preliminary letter about the book to her publisher, noted the similarity to the Uncle Remus stories.[24] The primary debt of the former to the latter seems to be the presence of both rabbits and foxes in the story. But unlike the Uncle Remus stories, the rabbits here do not win by outsmarting either fox or badger. In fact, it is only a stroke of luck that distracts both predators, leading to their mutual destruction and the happenstance that permits the rescue of the rabbit babies. The badger is not a typical character in the Uncle Remus stories, and here the fox does not seem particularly wily. In fact, he has not been successful in capturing his prey for the day, and he concocts an elaborate plan in order to do in Tommy Brock, one that seems bound to fail from the beginning. The badger is the smart animal in this story, but his

easy accomplishment of the distracting of old Mr. Bouncer leads one
to question whether this prey is really a sufficient match for his mach-
inations. The climax features the happy ending of rabbit family reunited and safe at home, but the wily animals win nothing but the
chance to fight again. The Uncle Remus stories do tell of the triumph
of the powerless over the powerful, and in that way *The Tale of Mr. Tod*
is like the Uncle Remus tales, but the similarity ends there.

As Celia Catlett Anderson has noted, Beatrix Potter's fox stories owe
more to the medieval stories of Reynard the Fox than they do to Uncle
Remus.[25] Mr. Tod, like the fox of *Jemima Puddle-Duck,* is a gentleman,
as is Reynard. But in this story he does not have the opportunity for
civil and suave persuasion that he does in *Jemima.* Here, his good
breeding is evident in the fastidiousness of his housekeeping, with the
neat kitchen, the tablecloth, and clean bed linens that Tommy Brock
besmirches. He has a vast collection of crockery, some of it inherited
from "his grandmother, old Vixen Tod" (47), so that one can assume
his table is properly appointed, at least until his fight with Tommy
destroys every piece of china he might have inherited. Rather, it is
Tommy Brock who is the smooth-talking gentleman, with the ingratiating manner capable of hoodwinking old Mr. Bouncer. But his
housekeeping and personal hygiene are so deplorable that one does not
associate elegant manners with the badger.

It is only in the stories of Reynard that one finds the fox and badger
paired, both as menaces to the farmer, and, in the case of Reynard,
with the badger as his follower and supporter. One suspects from the
relationship of the two characters that they do not entertain as arch an
animosity as do foxes and rabbits or badgers and rabbits, for, as Anderson points out, Mr. Tod seems to tolerate, if not quite approve, of
the badger's subsequent occupation of his houses.[26] The fox does not
initially design to kill the badger, but rather to scare him off. That his
plan may have succeeded even better by killing the badger is a stroke
of good fortune, but in the end only the fox's home is destroyed, and,
as Potter says in the last line, the rabbits "had not waited long enough
to be able to tell the end of the battle between Tommy Brock and Mr.
Tod" (94). Her commentary in the present tense, as opposed to the
past tense of the narration for the rest of the story, that "there will
never be any love lost between Tommy Brock and Mr. Tod" (84) further
underscores the longstanding and perpetual nature of the enmity between the two.

Finally, as Anderson notes, it is Potter's acknowledgment, without design to mute or disguise, of the disagreeable side of nature that most clearly ties *The Tale of Mr. Tod* to the Reynard stories.[27] Animals have been eaten in this story, as evidenced by the presence of their bones in Mr. Tod's house. And Tommy Brock and Mr. Tod will both continue to exist, in order to harass the rabbits in the future. But like her frankness about the fate of Mr. Rabbit in Mrs. McGregor's pie in *Peter Rabbit,* Potter is unflinchingly truthful here, too. She describes the unpleasantness in detail, and the only time she judges her characters as less than honorable in their appetites is when she ironically comments on Tommy Brock's persiflage when he claims to eat baby rabbits only when he is otherwise deprived of sustenance, an eventuality that seems unlikely ever to happen, given his rotundity. Otherwise, her characters are simply living up to their animal nature in preying on each other. Mr. Tod is as justified as Mr. McGregor in chasing rabbits; it is simply the way of nature. It is the inevitability of such relationships, and Potter's willingness to explore them without reservation about the possible delicacy of her young audience, that makes her books seem all the more permanent and genuine to the child audience.

The pictures, too, underscore the mythic, permanent quality of the story. The many pen-and-ink sketches are framed by heavy black lines, and the lines in the pictures are equally heavy, with none of the delicacy one might have expected, given evidence of Potter's previous ability to draw the minute. Instead, the sketches are really more like drawings, with heavy, deliberate lines, and even more like woodcuts, in their hard, clear edges. These are not sketches quickly tossed off, as if Potter were only trying to satisfy her publishers and her public in their demands for her illustrations. Rather, they are deliberately planned in their boldness to give an antique, primitive quality to the story, one worthy of Caxton's woodcuts for his edition of Aesop's fables. The color pictures, though fewer, are not vignetted, nor are they surrounded by a heavy black line. Instead, each is framed with white space, but the backgrounds are so thoroughly colored that there is no chance of them fading into the color of the page. The pastels here are much lighter than those of the previous bunny books, especially in their green tones. This lightness contrasts with the boldness of the black lines in the pen-and-ink drawings and the density of the long blocks of print, so unusual in the Potter books. The lightness and prevalence of the green tones gives a sense of fading because of antiquity, and yet of permanence, as the greenness of nature is permanent and recurring in the cycle of seasons. The pictures are not featured as they are in other books and serve more as illustration rather than as pictures in picture books. But they are altogether consonant with Potter's overall design of the book and help to convey her message.

The Story of a Fierce Bad Rabbit

Beatrix Potter was as interested in other toys as she was in her books. A visit to her home in Near Sawrey reveals her collection of dolls and dollhouse artifacts. She was always concerned about the stuffed animals modeled after her characters, not only because they indicated an infringement on her copyright, but also because she wanted them to be true to her illustrations. She was no purist, either about her visual or verbal accomplishments. She began in 1906 to design a series of toy books for very young children, those who are barely verbal. The result was a trio of panoramic toy books: *The Story of a Fierce Bad Rabbit* (1906), *The Story of Miss Moppet* (1906), and *The Sly Old Cat* (1971). The three are characterized by the same species of animal characters Potter used elsewhere, terseness of text, and the panoramic form.

These panoramas were long strips of paper, on which the individual pages of pictures and text were arranged in order from left to right, the whole folded accordion-fashion and enclosed in a walletlike cover with a fold-over flap. The form must have seemed appropriate to Potter. It was another kind of book, more like a toy than a story. Potter was unusually willing, for an author with such decided views about her books, to use the pictures in other forms that are not strictly literary. Thus, she made painting books and greeting cards, wallpaper and appointment books, where the pictures are simply decorations. But the panoramas were not popular with booksellers because of the difficulty of folding the books back into their covers once they had been unfolded by curious customers. In 1906 *The Story of a Fierce Bad Rabbit* and *The Story of Miss Moppet* were first issued in the panoramic form. *The Sly Old Cat* was scheduled for publication the next year. The first two were later reissued in a size slightly smaller than the usual Potter books, and today are included in the Peter Rabbit series in standard size and cover. The last book succumbed to the pressures from booksellers not to send any more of those cumbersome little toys, and so was not published until after Potter's death. Consequently, it is not included in the standard Peter Rabbit series of books.

That the stories are simplified to the point of hardly being stories at all is clear from Potter's use of the word "story" rather than "tale" in the titles. In an idiosyncratic way she defined a tale as narrative complicated by causality and extended plot as well as a variety of characters. Each of these panoramic narratives is really a vignette, composed of no more than three characters, of whom one is clearly dominant. The characters are also paired according to archetypical animosities: rabbits and hunter in *A Fierce Bad Rabbit* and mouse and cat in *Miss Moppet* and *The Sly Old Cat*. In the case of all three it is the title character who dominates. In *A Fierce Bad Rabbit* the rabbit's fierceness is obvious from "his savage whiskers, and his claws and his turned-up tail."[28] That Potter is more interested in naming characters than in developing plot or personality is obvious from two aspects of her introduction of the rabbit: first, he has no clothes on and does not take any on throughout the story. Thus he can only be an animal and nothing more. Second, she deliberately directs the reader to observe the whiskers, claws, and tail, in order to recognize this subspecies of rabbit. The subsequent pages, containing the description of a "nice gentle rabbit" (10) and his carrot with no instruction to look at his features, nevertheless define the rabbit by his whiskers and claws, which are barely visible, and his tail, which is here used for sitting on. The specification of the carrot as a gift from the rabbit's mother tells where the carrot came from and separates the carrot as not being an identifying characteristic of rabbits who are gentle and nice.

The bad rabbit approaching in the background leads to the third picture, a confrontation of the two rabbits over the carrot, the fourth picture, showing the bad rabbit overcoming by brute force, and the fifth, showing the bad rabbit scratching the nice one. The picture of the hunter with the text, "This is a man with a gun" (20), again shows Potter's intention to name and designate in this book. She makes no assumptions about the child's previous familiarity with the animals and thus indicates the audience as particularly inexperienced. There is no elegant diction here, as in her books even for slightly older children, and consistently no more than one or two extremely short sentences on each page. That the gun will go off by the end of the story is almost a truism in theories of plot, and so it does, with the traditional onomatopoeia, "BANG!" (26). Here Potter indulges in none of the creative devising of onomatopoeia obvious in the "scritch-scratch" of *Peter Rabbit* or the "roly-poly" of *The Roly-Poly Pudding*. She deliberately hands the child the traditional sound, perhaps to instruct him about the most traditional uses of language.

That the gun should go off at the fierce bad rabbit rather than the nice gentle rabbit is also traditional and expected. After all, the nice gentle rabbit has already been scratched and hurt, both physically and emotionally, and deserves no more abuse. The line "This is what happens—" (29) accompanying the whirlwind of the fierce bad rabbit shot at, with tail visible at the same level as his ears, surrounded by a cloud of whiskers, does not graphically and grossly depict the blood and fur that might have resulted from a hunter's shot. Rather it simply suggests that the rabbit has lost himself, since the viewer cannot see the rabbit's body or face, but only the suggestive tumble. That he should have been shorn of whiskers and tail, those anatomical parts that define him as fierce and bad, is almost a necessity, in order to punish him adequately, and to give appropriate justice to the nice gentle rabbit who is looking on.

The brevity of text and the simplicity of pictures, with none of the woodland detail that Potter so capably executed elsewhere, shows her instinctive grasp of her audience's limited capabilities in distinguishing figure from background. But that she does include background shows not only her preference for such composition in her drawings, but also an awareness that children prefer pictures that show depth. Most of the pictures show full frontal views or profile views, which help delineate the major defining features of the figures. Her description of the pictures in the text, with no intent to have the illustrations comment ironically on the text, indicates the simple "story" she designed to tell, rather than the "tale" she wrote elsewhere.

The "baby" book was an interesting diversion for Potter and shows what she could accomplish in that genre, but the creations are none of her best. They show how far she could strip down her artistic and literary styles, and how much story and character can be distilled in very few sentences and pictures. But Potter is much more accomplished when she has a plot to deal with and character with some depth. Her books reach their height of accomplishment when she has an actual place for the setting, rather than the generalized, unspecific backgrounds of these panorama books. Her lack of understanding about babies is clearly indicated by her use of the panoramic form. Babies find paper, even when bound into book form, wonderfully pliable and fit for mutilation. For the very young, the only joy in a book is turning the pages; they do not read, so much as they "do" a book. The panorama offers a long strip of paper easy to despoil but difficult to experience as a book. Indeed, the form relies on the convention of reading from left to right along the strip of paper, a convention that the very young have not yet encountered. In fact, without a binding to associate with the left side of a book, the panorama may seem equally intelligible upside down as right side up to the very young child, and the flap on the wallet may be as interesting as any other part of the book.

Few books for such young children endure from generation to generation, and writers, publishers, and illustrators are only now beginning to address the issue of quality and appropriateness for the very young. Potter's *Peter Rabbit* and other books that she wrote for the slightly older pre-reader, one who is able to understand some of the rudiments about books and illustrations, are a great legacy from Potter. The panoramic books, perpetuated by inclusion in the Peter Rabbit series, are a good start at an infant's library and introduction to the world of Potter's animal fantasy.

Chapter Three
Mice, Squirrels, and Other "Rubbish" Animals

Beatrix Potter always maintained that the animals about which she wrote were "rubbish"[1]—that is, not that they were worthless, but that they were expendable, not livestock or "working" animals. They were pets of one sort or another, and as such they could be carefully observed and studied without interrupting their purpose in life. In fact, these animals have no real purpose other than to survive and to give humans the pleasure and amusement of observing them. Potter's most felicitous and successful animal creations are her mice, who lend themselves easily to characterization and social behavior similar to humans. Though squirrels are near relatives of mice, Potter's imagination did not succeed with them very well, perhaps because squirrels are wild animals who do not live in close confines with human beings. Their intractability as pets made them less moldable in Potter's mind, and thus her two squirrel stories are some of her less satisfactory. This chapter examines in detail a wide assortment of Potter animals, to evaluate her re-creation of them in her fantasy world and the sources of her successes and failures with them.

The Tailor of Gloucester

Beatrix Potter always maintained that *The Tailor of Gloucester* (1903) was her favorite book. The story is a fairy tale that takes place in Gloucester at some time in the unknown past when fabrics "had strange names, and were very expensive."[2] The Lord Mayor of Gloucester has commissioned the tailor to make him a coat and a vest—called a "waistcoat" in the story—to be finished by Christmas Day, in time for the mayor's wedding. The tailor realizes that the commission is a very special one and will make his fortune, but the deadline for finishing the work is drawing close, and there is only a four-pence piece between the tailor and destitution. The tailor has been thrifty in cutting out the garment, so careful that he has hardly any scraps left over. But the four pence must last him for food and supplies from Tuesday until Saturday.

When he returns home after cutting out the gaments, he sends his cat Simpkin to purchase food with the first three pence and with the last penny to buy just enough thread to finish the last buttonhole. Without the thread the tailor will not be able to finish the waistcoat, and he will lose the payment he expects from the Lord Mayor's order. But while he waits for the cat to return, he hears peculiar scratching noises in the kitchen cupboard among the pieces of china. As he searches in the cupboard for the source of the noise, he inadvertently frees the mice whom Simpkin had caught and imprisoned under inverted teacups, to be saved for the cat's supper. When Simpkin returns, he is angry with the tailor for releasing his dinner, and he will not answer whether he has purchased the buttonhole thread.

The tailor falls sick for three days, ill with a fever and mumbling the whole time about the buttonhole thread and its importance to his project. On Christmas Eve Simpkin, thin and worried about his master, goes out into the streets of Gloucester and finds himself in the middle of human carolers and animal rhymers, who, according to the Christmas Eve tradition, are granted the gift of speech for that one special night. As he nears the tailor's shop, he hears the squeak of mouse voices and sounds of shears snipping and threads breaking. But the mice will not let him into the shop, and they close the shutters in his face.

On Christmas morning Simpkin is penitent about the mental anguish he has caused his master and places in the man's hands the buttonhole thread purchased and yet kept secret. The tailor, still weak, goes to his shop to do what he can about completing the Lord Mayor's coat and vest before noon, the time of the wedding. When he opens the door, he finds both garments finished, except for the last buttonhole on the vest, to which there is pinned a small note about the lack of thread. The Lord Mayor has his wedding suit in time, and the tailor's luck changes. From then on, he has many commissions from wealthy gentlemen, and the neatness and careful stitches of his buttonholes are widely esteemed to be "*so* small" that "they looked as if they had been made by little mice!" (59).

The Tailor of Gloucester is a very different work from *Peter Rabbit*. One suspects that those readers who had come to expect another rabbit adventure found *The Tailor* disappointing because the animals are involved in none of the drama of human-animal interaction. Although the mice in the story are in some peril from the tailor's cat, it seems unlikely that the cat will do anything more than worry them. The mice are not as daring as Peter; after all, they are supporters of the tailor, not his enemies.

The story is also a fairy tale, unlike *Peter Rabbit,* which more closely resembles a beast fable, and where the writer assumes a realistic, commonsense tone of narration. The events of the story presume an intimate, reciprocal relationship between humans and animals: Simpkin is more than a cat, he is nursemaid and companion. The mice are not verminous intruders, at least not to the tailor; they are the architects of the tailor's and Simpkin's ultimate good fortune. The story bears a resemblance to the Grimm brothers' "The Elves and the Shoemaker," in which a well-intentioned cobbler spends the last of his money on just enough leather for a pair of shoes. Because the man is good-hearted, elves come in the night and make the shoes for him. Their craftsmanship is so extraordinary that the shoes sell for a very good price, and the shoemaker has enough money to buy leather for more shoes, which he cuts out and which the elves finish for him.

Like many fairy tales, Potter's story presents a lesson to be learned. In both *The Tailor of Gloucester* and "The Elves and the Shoemaker" the artisan is good-hearted, thrifty, and skillful. Some magical force outside his own efforts rewards his virtues and changes his fortune for the better. The Christmas setting in *The Tailor* gives the tale a religious aura not found in any other Potter book. Likewise, in "The Elves and the Shoemaker" the cobbler says his prayers before he goes to sleep, leaving the impression that the cobbler is rewarded at least partly for his proper religious attitude and reliance on God. In neither story do the magical elements seem divinely inspired; neither mice nor elves leave messages of high import after they have done their work. But in each story the moral seems to be that hard work and generosity pay off, even if magic must intervene to effect the reward for those who deserve it.

It is easy to see why Beatrix Potter preferred *The Tailor of Gloucester* over her other books; both the story and the drawings permitted her to dwell on subjects for which she felt a particular affection. The fairy-tale genre was one that had appealed to her from childhood, though she seldom indulged herself in such tales in her books. The pictures of the mice show them posed in particularly playful attitudes, dressed in the antique clothing that had attracted her attention in the Victoria and Albert Museum. The detail of the china in the cupboard, of the mantlepiece before which the tailor warms and rests himself, of the old buildings and narrow passageways in the old city of Gloucester, were all subjects that Potter had found particularly fascinating and that she had sketched repeatedly over the years.

The human figure of the tailor, because he is seldom seen as the focal point of the illustrations, and because she did not pose him in full frontal view, did not give her the problems that she had in drawing humans such as Mr. McGregor in *Peter Rabbit*. The world of the mice, living in the walls of the old city, existing harmoniously among themselves with little interference from the humans who might otherwise have interrupted their lives, the exquisite delicacy of the embroidery on the garments she used as models, the elegant, antique finery of the mice when she draws them clothed, all required Potter to exercise extreme care and her ability to draw the exquisitely delicate details of her miniature fantasy world. The fact that the story is set in some remote past only heightened her pleasure in creating this world in her illustrations.

Sources. Potter first heard the story in 1894, while visiting her cousin's home in Stroud, just outside of Gloucester. The original legend concerned a local tailor named Prichard, who was commissioned by the new Lord Mayor of Gloucester to make him a waistcoat to wear to the opening of the local agricultural show, his first duty as the new Lord Mayor. Prichard was worried about finishing the waistcoat in time, and his assistants, knowing of his concern, worked secretly over the weekend to finish the project. When Prichard returned on Monday to find the waistcoat finished except for the last buttonhole, he hung a sign in the window reading "Come to Prichard where the waistcoats are made at night by the fairies."[3] This tailor was still living in Gloucester at the time that Potter first visited, and she saw his shop and sketched it, even at that early date turning the hot, summer scene before her into snow-clad winter. She also set it in the past, at a time when Lord Mayors were more important than simple figureheads, and when elegant clothing and fabrics were works of art. Potter's inspiration to turn the fairies into sewing mice suited her conception about the animal world where creatures were as capable as humans of showing gratitude and performing human activities. It also suited her fascination about mice, who were her earliest pets and whom she had observed closely and sketched constantly from her earliest days as an apprentice artist.

Her first solo visit to Gloucester was an extraordinary one, not only because she found the inspiration for the book she would someday write and illustrate, but also because it was one of the first visits she made unaccompanied by either parent. From time to time she returned for more visits and continued to sketch buildings and streets in Gloucester, as if unconsciously collecting material for the book, and declaring, through both book and journey, her eventual independence from her parents.

In 1901, after she had published *Peter Rabbit* on her own, she wrote the original manuscript of *The Tailor of Gloucester* in a school exercise book, and gave it to Noel Moore's younger sister Freda as a Christmas gift. The original version was much longer, with many more rhymes and carols sung by the talking animals on Christmas Eve, and fewer illustrations. Because the text is so much longer than most of her other books, and because the illustrations were so few—only twelve for the total manuscript—the language seems much more noteworthy in *The Tailor* than in some of her other, shorter books.

Potter found obvious delight in the many long, foreign, and obsolete English words describing the kinds of fabric and clothing that elegant people wore in the tailor's time, as evidenced by her glossary of fabric terms in Freda Moore's manuscript. And in Freda's original manuscript one sees more clearly than elsewhere in Potter's work the influence of the Old Testament and the works of Shakespeare. Potter appears to have borrowed from both sources particular parts of antique, even obsolete syntax. For example, in the manuscript, when the tailor sends Simpkin out to make his purchases, he charges the cat, "But lose not the last penny of the four-pence Simpkin, or I am undone. . . ."[4] It is apparent from the revisions she made in the first, privately printed edition of *The Tailor* that she recognized the odd sound of the construction "lose not," for she alters it to read, "do not lose."[5] But even under the careful editorship of Norman Warne, she kept the phrase "I am undone" rather than alter it to read something like "I have been undone" or "you will undo me," partly because the construction is more direct, with fewer words, and partly because it harmonizes with the archaic use of the word "undone" to mean utterly destroyed rather than to mean simply unfinished.

Elsewhere in the final Warne edition Potter shows her pleasure in antique phrasing—for example, "One-and-twenty button-holes," "This is passing extraordinary!" (25), and "I am worn to a ravelling" (53), the tailor's apt description of his emotional state in terms of his craft. Her memory of nursery rhymes and her own facility at rhyming are clear in the many rhymes that survived even Norman Warne's economical cuts. In reading the rhymes, the reader recognizes their origins in J. O. Halliwell's *Nursery Rhymes of England,* and in Walter Crane's *The Baby's Opera* and *The Baby's Bouquet.* But though the rhymes may sound familiar, the Potter versions add a novel twist to what the reader expects, which makes the rhymes new and not at all like a compilation of worn, old favorites, even in the rather lengthy collection in the manuscript version of *The Tailor.* For example, "Little Miss Muffet" sitting on her tuffet, combines with "Little Jack Horner" sitting in his corner, to become

> Little Poll Parrot
> Sat in a garret
> Eating toast and tea!
> A little brown mouse,
> Jumped into his house
> and stole it all away!
> (*0* 48)

By taking the original nursery rhymes and preserving their expected rhythms and narrative patterns—the initial figure seated, and in the case of Miss Muffet, visited by an intruder who completely disrupts the scene—and yet shifting the action to animals, especially the brown mouse who resembles so closely the magic mice of the story, Potter makes the rhyme her own.

Revisions. Potter assumed that her publishers would not be interested in another project from her so soon after having taken on *Peter Rabbit,* and certainly not before the first book had proved its commercial success. So, in the same month that she published *Peter Rabbit* on her own, Warne decided to publish the book with colored illustrations in the next year, and Potter wrote the original version of *The Tailor of Gloucester.* Fearing that her publishers would ask her to cut many of her favorite rhymes, she decided to publish *The Tailor of Gloucester* on her own, with some added illustrations, and most of the earlier ones redrawn. She went to the museum to find models for the Lord Mayor's coat and vest, and for the elegant wardrobes of the mice. She visited a tailor's shop, and while the man was busy sewing a button back on her coat, she sketched him in the tailor's traditional cross-legged posture, bent over his work.

The process of revision, from the manuscript, through her privately printed edition, to the edition Warne finally published in 1903, mirrors the process Potter went through with *Peter Rabbit*. The manuscript, though more thoughtfully designed as a book than was the original Peter Rabbit letter, shows a certain lack of attention to the text. The paragraphs are lengthy and sometimes repetitive. In her revision for her own edition she divided up many of the paragraphs into new ones of only one or two sentences. She made this revision because of the appearance of the longer paragraphs on the pages of the exercise book, which were larger than the miniature format she chose for the first edition. A long paragraph on such a small page would have meant a solid block of text with little white space. The format looks crowded and difficult to read when the page is small and completely filled with printing. The revisions also have the effect of making the text easier to read and more comprehensible for younger readers. Potter early noted that children aged twelve were particularly likely to read and enjoy *The Tailor*.[6] The revision of paragraph length would have made the book more accessible and comprehensible to these younger readers, even though twelve-year-olds may be more competent with longer paragraphs than Potter assumed.

She also paid more attention to conventional punctuation when she revised the manuscript for publication. Her manuscripts are characterized by many dashes and exclamation marks, as if she did not seriously consider punctuation and its effect on the text while she was composing. In the actual books she usually slowed the pace of the text by using dashes more sparingly and inserting commas to set off phrases. This added punctuation not only slows the pace of the text, but also makes the grammar of the sentences more obvious, by setting off appositives, relative clauses, and items in series.

In the case of *The Tailor*, unlike the revision of *Peter Rabbit*, her task was to compress the story in revision, rather than lengthen it by adding motivation. The most obvious cuts come in the nursery rhymes that the animals sing on Christmas Day before daylight. Norman Warne's advice about cutting the number of rhymes and their length was sound. In the original manuscript, and even in the privately printed edition, the rhymes ramble on, with no particular organization. The surfeit of rhymes was included because of Potter's particular affection for them. For her, the manuscript's most important audience was herself; she included all the rhymes because they pleased her, not because they helped to build suspense or foreshadowing, or to extend the story's motifs. She also considered the Moore children as an important audience. But through their personal acquaintance with her, they had come to enjoy her many parodies and recastings of traditional rhymes so that she could count on them to suspend critical judgment about the rhymes.

However, as she suspected when she decided to publish the book on her own first rather than show it to Warne, her publishers were more objective about the rhymes. Those that remain are mainly about cats or mice, the principal characters of the story, or are Christmas carols, to help maintain a sense of time and setting, or are about tailoring, the primary activity of both humans and mice in the story. The remaining rhymes do not interrupt the story. Instead they serve to aid its development thematically and are not so long that the story turns into a collection of rhymes, permitting the reader to forget that the story is a fairy tale. The process of shifting the narrative from traditional sources to her own original inspirations is one clear direction in her writing suggested by Norman Warne. Potter also willingly acceded to Harold Warne's suggestion of cutting out a picture of the mice making merry in the tailor's basement, complete with the mice drinking from a bottle of liquor. Though in later years Potter remonstrated that Harold Warne was too worried about offending the public, at this point in her career she worked hard to accommodate her publishers, even Harold Warne, whom she later learned to deal with more forcefully.

Motivation

Potter also clarifies considerably the motivation of mice and cat in the story, again widening the audience to those readers who cannot jump to conclusions based on the rather scanty evidence of motivation in the original manuscript. In the original story it only gradually becomes clear that the mice are trapped in various pieces of crockery because Simpkin is saving them for his meals. How they get into the shop, how they know what the tailor needs done on the Lord Mayor's garments, why they decide to go to work in the first place are motivations only implied.

Though she moves in the direction of greater explanation in the first edition, it was not until Norman Warne read that edition and began to help Potter shape it that motivation is truly clarified. In the Warne edition the mice of Gloucester are described as having their own civilization living within the walls and in secret passageways underneath the streets and in the old buildings: "For behind the wooden wainscots of all the old houses in Gloucester, there are little mouse staircases and secret trap-doors; and the mice run from house to house through those long narrow passages; they can run all over the town without going into the streets" (17). When the tailor locks his shop and leaves for the night, he thinks he leaves it empty, but Potter explains that the shop is not as deserted as he assumes: "No one lived there at night but little brown mice, and they run in and out without any keys!" (14). So the mice defy both Simpkin and the tailor by using their secret transit system. They thus have easy access to the tailor's workplace.

Even in the original manuscript, the idea of mice in the shop is suggested at the beginning of the story, when the tailor so carefully cuts his fabrics that the scraps are too small for anything "except waist-coats—for mice" (O 12). But Potter makes the mice physically and more obviously present in the final version: they remain behind in the shop even though the tailor has left. They also remain behind to listen to him after he has liberated them and saved them from Simpkin's dinner plans. They know the answer to the tailor's rhetorical question, "Was it right to let loose those mice, undoubtedly the property of Simpkin?" (29). In their gratitude, they will not let the tailor come to disaster, about which he keeps worrying even in his fevered sickbed, and they learn about his exact plans for the coat and vest by listening to his fitful, preoccupied mutterings. It is clear in the Warne edition that the mice leave the tailor's house only the first night of the story and bring all their friends with them to the shop to help them sew. The final version also makes clear that the garments are not an over-night miracle wrought by special powers given to the mice on Christmas Eve. The laborers have been sewing all week, and the high spirits Simpkin observes among them in the shop on Christmas Eve are simply the culmination of three days' hard and careful work.

Simpkin's motivation is also clearer in the final version. In the man-uscript he returns from his shopping trip covered with snow and net-tled at least partly because of his dampness. That he has hidden the buttonhole thread is implied when he sniffs around the china cupboard and when "he slipped a little packet into the tea-pot, and looked an-grily at the tailor" (O 23). He continues to make horrid noises through-out the night while the tailor suffers in his illness. His gradual development of sympathy for the tailor is clear, but his change of heart can only be inferred in the manuscript.

In the final version Potter clearly states that "he felt quite ashamed of his badness compared with those good little mice!" (50). Potter also edits the scene when the tailor wakes up from his illness so that Simpkin's transformation is more emphatically and clearly the focus. The crucial line in the original manuscript reads, "Beside his bed stood the repentant Simpkin with a cup of tea and the last of the sausages, fizzling hot upon a pewter plate" (O 59). In this version the line trails off to focus on the food and Simpkin's self-sacrifice in giving it to the tailor rather than eating it himself. In the privately printed edition Potter tries once again to focus the line more clearly: ". . . and beside his bed stood the repentant Simpkin with a cup of tea!"[7] The distraction of the sausages is gone, but the exclamation point emphasizes the tea rather than the cat; the emphasis is misplaced. In the Warne edition the line is finally edited down to its most crucial components, and the emphasis finally falls where it belongs: ". . . and beside his bed stood the repentant Simpkin!" (50). The gesture of the cup of tea is clear in the illustration accompanying the text, but the exclamation point is placed where it belongs, to emphasize that this is really the climax of the story; from here follows the denouement.

Both manuscript and private edition dwell on street and place names in Gloucester, as if Potter were indulging herself in a kind of travelogue of places and sights in the city which she had enjoyed visiting and sketching. However, details about the snow falling on the cathedral and the Lord Mayor's dog joining in the animal chorus on Christmas Eve focus the story too clearly on Gloucester. These details give the story a particularity of location that fights against the universality of the fairy-tale genre, the Christmas story, and the moral about showing gratitude. The tailor may have lived anywhere. The setting in Gloucester, a city with a history from Roman times and therefore a locale filled with legends, gives the story its antique quality, just as the setting of a fairy tale "once upon a time" in any period but the present and in any place other than the reader's own location places the story in an indefinite past and indefinite place. So placing the story in Gloucester gives it distance in time and place from most readers. Dwelling too much on the realistic details of Gloucester in Potter's own time violates the sense of mythic omnipresence that the story otherwise conveys

Though some such details remain in the Warne edition, they are not intrusive, and in some ways serve to develop the verisimilitude of the story, the sense "that it is true—at least about the tailor, the waistcoat, and the 'No more twist!'" (7), as Potter says in the dedication to Freda Moore. Westgate Street, the location of the tailor's shop, is not so particular a name that it limits the setting only to Gloucester, and the presence of the cathedral and the college in the story serve to create a sense of a large, significant city of culture and beauty, one that has been around long enough to have developed a history where legends like this might thrive. The cathedral clock, marking the beginning of the animals' time for singing with its chimes, lends a feeling of solemnity, for the legend about the talking animals derives from the Christmas story itself in which according to tradition the beasts of burden at the manger were granted the gift of speech. Potter records many visits to cathedrals, churches, and chapels during her many vacation trips, and the impressiveness of those buildings for her. Her sense of the sacred presence of the church presiding over the city is clear in the story, but not in such a way that such a relationship between city and church could exist only in Gloucester.

   Illustrations.   The final area in which Potter made major changes was in the specialized vocabulary about clothing and fabrics. In her research for the Warne edition she went to the Victoria and Albert Museum to use the clothing in the museum's collection for her pictures. There she found models for the coat and waistcoat, which she copied so meticulously that when one compares the embroidery stitches on the waistcoat to the individual strands of thread shown in her drawings, the two match almost stitch for stitch. Here she had actual models, not simply imagined clothing; so the descriptions of the garments changed to match. The original manuscript describes the waistcoat as made "of peach-coloured satin, worked with thread of gold and silver" and the coat as decorated with "embroidery upon the cuffs and upon the pocket flaps and upon the skirts of the coat . . ."(O 62). In her revision for the first edition Potter added that the vest had rosebuds embroidered upon it.[8] But with an exact model in front of her she could be more specific and expansive in the final edition: "There were roses and pansies upon the facings of the coat; and the waistcoat was worked with poppies and corn-flowers" (56). Because her model vest was cream-colored, so became the vest in the story. Because it was actually "trimmed with gauze and green worsted chenille" (12–13), it is so described in the text.

   Because these garments originated in a particular historical period, late eighteenth century, she altered the tailor's vocabulary accordingly. His scraps become "tippets for mice and ribbons for mobs" in the final

Warne edition (13). The illustration accompanying the text at that point shows a lady mouse dressed in an eighteenth-century gown, wearing a mobcap trimmed with ribbons, to emphasize not only the historical period, but also the clearly imagined quality of the tailor's fantasy. The revisions also clarify the meanings of the obsolete terms. Because of her research, she changed the "tobine stripes" of embroidery upon the vest in the original manuscript (*O* 19) to "tabby stripes" in the private edition,[9] to "tambour stitch" in the Warne edition (25). And finally, because she had done her research and sketched a number of authentic interiors for her pictures, she could specify that the china cupboard was filled with "crockery and pipkins, willow pattern plates, and tea-cups and mugs" (22), which were more typical of and specific to period than "cracked plates and crockery, and pie-dishes and pipkins, and grey-beard mugs and pewter plates" as described in the manuscript (*O* 18).

In all, Potter's revisions make the story much clearer and consistent in historical specificity, while at the same time more universal in setting by cutting the story loose from its historical origins in Gloucester. The motivation for the events in the story is clearer, the narrative more compact, the story altogether more carefully crafted and focused than the original manuscript or the privately printed edition.

In revising and adding to her illustrations for the private edition, Potter used many of the pictures in the original manuscript, but redrew all ten of the original twelve, giving a clearer sense of finished drawing and less the appearance of quick sketch. By the time she was preparing the Warne edition, her drawings were more specific and detailed. The lady mouse appearing from under the teacup has a clearly painted mobcap, apron, petticoat, and pumps, and her teacup has a clear pattern and outline, rather than being suggestively sketched as simple background, as in the manuscript. Potter's interiors of the tailor's shop and his room are filled with details of architecture and furnishing missing in the original manuscript, and there is, obviously, more detail about the garments the tailor and mice are working on. Simpkin is more clearly a tiger cat, and even the snow-covered city seems colder and darker than in the original sketches.

In the original manuscript Potter simply vignetted the pictures. That is, she surrounded them with white space, in a suggestive oval. The reproductions of the original manuscript seem to suggest that the paper she used was not white, but cream-colored or ivory, which lends a feeling of antiquity and age to the illustrations. When she drew the pictures for the Warne edition, she surrounded each picture with a black line, forming pictures in uniform square blocks. In her correspondence with her publishers she was clearly upset at the printer's error in trimming off this outline, which she had added, she said, "to make the snow in the foreground look white. It is quite certain to look dirty against a white margin." As she noted in the same letter, "the black frame pulls them together and sends back the distance."[10] By setting the pictures off from the white of the page Potter was able to use shading more effectively, to use whites that are not quite so white as the page to lend to the pictures the sensations of the glow of candlelight and fire, and the luminescence of snow-covered landscape as seen at night.

These methods of lighting are no longer seen so prevalently. Nighttime skies are no longer as dark as they once were, given the abundance of electric light even in isolated areas. And candle and fire light are much yellower and less harsh than either incandescent or fluorescent illumination. By being able to set the picture off from the page with the frame Potter could more clearly portray these lighting effects and give to her illustrations some of the yellowed, antique quality that the exercise-book paper gave to the original manuscript. And the pictures do, in fact, give the illusion of some depth when surrounded by the frame.

Finally, the uniformity and consistency of the frames make the pictures seem more important and more carefully preserved than the vignetted pictures either of the original manuscript or even of *Peter Rabbit*. The frame gives a sense of historical record, of pictures framed because they are an important, accurate portrayal of an actual event. Because of the frames, the pictures have a sense of historical importance, as do framed pictures in a gallery, and give the story's record a kind of permanent importance, as if to underscore the assertion in Potter's foreword that the story "is true,"especially "the tailor, the waistcoat, and the 'No more twist!'" (7).

Of all of Potter's books this one is the most romantic and fantastic. Though it shows none of the hardheaded realism of her other successful books, yet it still succeeds, partly because the animals are so carefully drawn and realized. Cats and mice were some of Potter's earliest pets, and mice in particular lend themselves to human clothing and postures. Though the fairy tales of Potter's retirement, especially *The Fairy Caravan*, are verbose and lacking in tension, such is not the case here. One suspects that Norman Warne's careful criticism kept the book from going in the same direction as *The Fairy Caravan* and that the illustrations, tapping as they do Potter's love of antiques and of fine detail, also kept her aware of her tendencies toward long, romantic descriptions.

The Tale of Squirrel Nutkin

The idea of squirrels using their tails as sails had first occurred to Beatrix Potter as early as 1897, when she wrote to Noel Moore about an American story of squirrels sailing across a river. Though Linder identifies two possible sources for such a story,[11] it is equally possible that the source was some American folktale about squirrels, perhaps from an American Indian source. In 1901, when she was again on summer vacation with her parents at Lingholm, near Keswick in the Lake District, she heard from one of the residents of the presence of squirrels on an island when the nuts were ripe. She proceeded to wonder, in a letter to Norah Moore, how the squirrels arrived on the island to do their collecting.

After she published *The Tailor of Gloucester* privately and Warne had accepted it for publication, she turned her mind to another book to be published in the same year, one without rabbits, cats, or mice. The holiday and the presence of the squirrels gathering nuts in the early autumn led her to *The Tale of Squirrel Nutkin* (1903) whose story had originated in the picture letter to Norah Moore. The availability of landscape for sketching, including an island on Derwentwater which she appropriated for use as Owl's Island in the book, and the squirrels around her holiday site to serve as models, all factors made the book an easy one to take in hand.

The story concerns one squirrel, the eponymous hero who has an uncharacteristically short tail, and the circumstances surrounding the loss of part of his tail. The squirrels, using their tails as sails, cross over the water to Owl Island, which is owned and dominated by an owl named Old Brown, the terror of squirrels. Though the other squirrels deferentially ask permission of Old Brown to gather nuts, a request he silently grants, Squirrel Nutkin taunts Old Brown with riddles and chants, with respect neither for Old Brown's position on the island nor his ability to do with Squirrel Nutkin what he will. This pattern recurs for six days, at the end of which Old Brown is so exasperated with Nutkin's impertinence that he captures him in preparation for skinning and devouring him. But Nutkin makes a last-minute escape, leaving behind, as a kind of punishment, the greater part of his tail between Old Brown's talons.

The story is at least partly a *pourquoi* story, one which explains the presence of an occasional short-tailed red squirrel, and the kinds of natural disasters occurring in a squirrel's life that might had led to such a mutilation without the loss of life. The story also explains what squirrels are saying when they chatter, and why squirrels chatter back and throw things on humans who presume to talk to them. In this way, the story becomes a sort of legend, with a feeling of folktale and tradition to it.

Nutkin is also the closest Beatrix Potter comes in her books to the kind of wildlife study typical in the books of Ernest Thompson Seton. Seton studied animal behaviors and habitats and wrote about them in order to contribute to a child's knowledge of natural history, but without attempting to personify the animal or tell a consistent story about him. Neither the squirrels nor the owl in this story wear clothes. The closest to human behavior they get is Old Brown's habit of using human utensils to eat his honey off a plate. In the main, the squirrels are squirrels, except for the opening fantasy about their sailing by using their tails. They do converse with Old Brown and walk single file, in uncharacteristically human orderliness. Nutkin is given to dancing on his hind legs. But Potter's animals here are at their least human, primarily because they live in their natural habitats and do not wear clothes. Nutkin's .ed tail holds the same kind of significance for him that Peter Rabbit's blue jacket does for the bunny. But Nutkin's tail is a defining part of his anatomy, and not an artificial covering, as is Peter's jacket.

Potter's one attempt at humanization here is in the riddles that Nutkin uses to taunt Old Brown. Nutkin asks riddles, but, for Potter, his behavior also explains what squirrels chatter about in their own language. Thus, the riddling is both human and animal. Riddling is part of an ancient pattern in folktales, and the contest of riddles, where the winner is the one who can stump his competitor, is designed to show the hero's superior intelligence, not only in using clues and figuring out answers but also in making up riddles to stymie his opponent. Riddles are also enticing to children, especially given the capacity of riddling to stump and exasperate adults.

In this story Nutkin's use of riddles makes him childlike, in his rapid, chattering speech and his playful disregard for the serious consequences of his actions. Old Brown, in his silent, but powerful and brooding presence over the island, is the adult. Old Brown refuses to play the game with Nutkin, but the child who hears the riddles can play, and can derive from answering a sense of mastery over Old Brown and, by symbolic displacement, over other adults.

For the reader who is not British the rhymes may seem particularly obscure, but if the reader takes hints from the text, the answers easily reveal themselves. The "little wee man, in a red red coat"[12] is a red squirrel. "Hitty Pitty" (25) is the nettle with which Nutkin is tickling Old Brown. "A house full, a hole full" (26) refers to the nuts Nutkin is gathering. The "bonny swine" (38) are bumblebees. And the "Humpty Dumpty" rhymes (45) taunt Old Brown with ruining the egg that the other squirrels have given him as a propitiating offering. "Hickamore, Hackamore" (49) and "Arthur O'Bower" (50) both refer to the pesky presence of the taunting squirrel, and what he thinks is Old Brown's inability to get rid of him. "Flour of England, fruit of Spain" (34) is obscure, but may refer to raisins, or plums as they are called in England, which are like the beetles that the squirrels have just offered Old Brown; or perhaps the riddle refers to plum pudding itself.

Potter gives many hints to her riddles, and in one case even gives away the answer, as with "How many strawberries grow in the sea?" "As many herrings as grow in the wood" (33). The rhymes, with some changes, are, as Potter claims in the book, "as old as the hills," for they are all traditional nursery rhymes that British children would know and other readers can easily guess from the context. But Old Brown will not participate, even though the child reader does. And whether he knows the answers or not, his exasperation with Nutkin and the squirrel's impertinence in asking riddles in the first place, and then complicating his misstep with tickling the owl in falsely assumed familiarity and shouting to him through the keyhole, all suggest a moralistic, punitive end to the squirrel that the reader feels is deserved.

Potter here is being uncharacteristically judgmental. Though Nutkin is a sympathetic character, the reader does not sympathize with him wholly, the way he does with Peter Rabbit. Nutkin shows bad manners and foolhardiness about the consequences of his lack of etiquette. The reader's ability to answer his riddles gives a further feeling of superiority. The harshness of the justice is mitigated by the fact that Nutkin is permitted to live and by the lack of ridicule from the other squirrels. But Potter's failure to imagine the squirrel as more thoroughly human, combined with her punitive justice, fail to draw upon her finer abilities in writing and make *Nutkin* one of her less successful stories.

The pictures suffer from what Potter feared would be the problem with *Peter Rabbit*—a prevalence of natural colors with insufficient contrast to keep them from becoming routine. In *Peter Rabbit* the pictures are rescued by the rabbits' clothing, especially the contrast of Peter's blue jacket with the rest of the natural setting. In *Nutkin* Potter had no such device to save the pictures from sameness. The squirrels are virtually identical, with little delineation of facial features among them and only Nutkin's high-stepping antics to set him apart from his kin. The story also has little to say about human beings in general and is pointed rather directly at naughty, intrusive children. Thus *Nutkin* does not draw on Potter's acute observations of human relations, but rather stoops rather didactically to talk to children. The reliance on the riddles, away from which Norman Warne gradually steered Potter, is still obvious here, and though Potter found pleasure in them, the reader gradually finds them tedious.

The Tale of Two Bad Mice

Beatrix Potter had already written and published a mouse book, *The Tailor of Gloucester,* with Warne and was concerned about publishing another so soon after the first. But in 1904 she was finishing up the drawings for *The Tale of Benjamin Bunny,* her second rabbit book, and admitted that she was "glad to get done with rabbits."[13] The mice she used for her models in *Two Bad Mice* (1904) were on hand, captured earlier during the sketching trip for *The Tailor of Gloucester,* and she knew of the doll's house that Norman Warne was building as a Christmas gift for his niece, the little girl to whom the story is dedicated.

Norman Warne conspired to bring the book about, first by building a glass house for the pet mice to live in, so that Potter could observe them in an interior scene and sketch them at the same time. He then offered photographs of the dollhouse when Mrs. Potter, sensing the growing intimacy between her daughter and the bachelor publisher, forbade further visits for her daughter to sketch the real house. When Potter requested dolls for the dollhouse, one a blond and the other a Dutch doll, Norman Warne filled her requests, thoughtfully sending the dolls rather than delivering them in person, and sending along with them some dollhouse food made of plaster. Both author and publisher took a great deal of interest and pleasure in the progress of the book. One suspects that the publisher was as indispensable in its creation as was the author-illustrator.

The story concerns the invasion of a dollhouse by the two mice while the dolls are not at home. Lucinda, the nominal owner of the house, and Jane, her cook and servant, live boring, decorative lives in the house. In contrast, the mice, more active and curious, find much that is interesting and useful in the house. While trying to eat the dollhouse food, they find it, to their disappointment and fury, to be inedible. In revenge, they take many of Lucinda's belongings for their own, go on a rampage and destroy the few furnishings that they do not appropriate for their own use.

When Lucinda and Jane return, they are horrified, and the little girl who owns the dollhouse resolves to get a policeman doll, whose implied purpose will be to keep the mice out in the future. The little girl's governess vows to set a trap, which is seemingly where the story ends. But Potter shows the mouse couple and their children looking at the trap, with the mouse parents presumably explaining to the children the dangers it portends. The coda to the story includes the restitution made by the mice for their damages by stuffing a scavenged sixpence in one of the stockings hung at the dollhouse chimney at Christmastime. The wife-mouse's return every morning to clean house for the dolls further ameliorates the animals' crimes.

For all the wanton destruction in this story, it is one of Potter's most lighthearted creations. The atmosphere is due at least in part to the smallness of the mice and the dollhouse, and the miniature scale of the havoc they wreak, which makes their burglaries and vandalism more laughable than serious. The dolls, though pretty, are necessarily lifeless and hard to sympathize with. Their stiffness contrasts with the lithe, quick movements of the mice and the animals' ability to discover the truth about the dolls' lives: they are all show and no substance. The line about the dolls' foodstuffs, "They would not come off the plates, but they were extremely beautiful,"[14] shows the sole criterion by which the dolls and dollhouse can be evaluated: by their capacity to please the sight with their decoration and in their miniature scale. The opening description of Lucinda, who never requests any meals for Jane to cook, and Jane, who consequently never does any cooking, sounds so unnatural, even for dolls, that the animals' disgust with the lack of substance in the food mirrors the reader's lack of sympathy for the dolls.

That the mice steal what is useful for themselves seems a much more

fitting use of the dollhouse furnishings. One can hardly feel sorry for
the dolls, whose expressions are so frozen that they cannot express any
horror when they return to the scene of the burglary. The lady mouse
needs the cradle she steals for the many little mice she is raising at
home, but Lucinda has no such offspring and no use for the cradle.
The dress the mouse steals for herself makes her look charming, but it
would not have had the same enchanting effect on the doll, who already
looks as good as she can. The theft of the bolster, so that the mice can
have their own feather bed, seems especially appropriate, since the
dolls cannot recline comfortably or recognize comfort anyway. The
mouse justifies her action to the reader because she has a good use for
her theft. It is true that the mice do become greedy when they try to
steal a bookcase and a birdcage, but they cannot fit either item into
their hole. So they mitigate their acquisitiveness by leaving the super-
fluity behind.

Margaret Blount has noted that nearly all mouse stories involve comparison of the mice and their feats to the human giants who dominate
their world.[15] It may come as a surprise to the reader of *Two Bad Mice*
that there is a little girl to whom the dollhouse belongs and that the
little girl has a governess. But there have been hints of the human
world throughout the book. The opening exterior view of the dollhouse
facing the first page of text shows that the scene is not set outside. The
wallpaper in the background and the carpet on which the dollhouse
sits betray the presence of humans, as do the jumprope and badminton
equipment surrounding the dollhouse. The human wallpaper may not
be nearly so evident in the deteriorated plates used in currently available editions, but it is much more clearly detailed and telling in earlier
issues. As Lucinda and Jane return from their outing, they are shown
arriving on the scene in a doll carriage. Though the text does not
mention a little girl at that time, the picture necessarily begs the question of who is pushing the carriage. When, on the next page, the
existence of the dollhouse owner is introduced in the text, the reader
who has already looked at the picture is not surprised.

The reader perceives that this little girl is just as imaginatively involved in the fantasy as the reader has been. Her solution to the mouse
invasion is another layer of fantasy. If the dolls are not mature enough
to care for themselves—and she has just shown her willingness to di-
minish them by treating them as her babies in the doll carriage—then
she need simply impose another doll who will. But the efficacy of her
solution is further brought into doubt when Potter presents a picture

of the policeman doll, so ridiculously tall that he cannot see the mice on the floor, and so stiff and precariously balanced that he could not chase them anyway. Of course, the governess introduces a note of ominous reality. The only way to deal with mice is to trap them. But the governess, like most adults who cling to reality and will not see the capabilities of animals in fantasy, underestimates the cleverness of the mice in evading the human, bloodthirsty intrusion. They are smart enough to avoid the trap, and they pass this intelligence and wisdom on to their children. Thus, though Potter prematurely announces, "So that is the story of the two Bad Mice" (56), she does so in an assumed adult, realistic voice, one not unlike, the reader suspects, the summary proclamation of the governess.

The story that proceeds after this announcement shows Potter's increasing willingness to defy the conventions of traditional storytelling. Though at the end of *Peter Rabbit* and *Benjamin Bunny* she slightly extends the story after the more obvious ending as the rabbits return home, she did not attach a lengthy coda to these stories to complicate them further. Rather, she introduced a simple denouement at the end of each to tie up loose ends. In *Two Bad Mice* Potter introduces loose ends that defy neat endings. The two mice subsequently atone for their misdeeds and are pronounced "not so very very naughty after all" (46), even though one suspects the sincerity of their atonement. The sixpence that they give to the dolls to pay for their breakage is a crooked one, and thus not legal tender. And the lady mouse's cleaning must not be terribly taxing, given the dolls' inactivity. The sight of the two mice stuffing the Christmas stocking while the dolls sleep parallels the animals with Father Christmas, another fantasy creation. The lady mouse's cleaning forays "very early every morning—before anybody is awake" (59) suggests two possibilities; either that she is not really cleaning at all, which is belied by the picture of her entering the house, capably wielding broom and dustpan; or that she is another creature of the night, like the sandman and the tooth fairy, which explains why dolls' houses are always so neat. Thus Potter defies the realistic ending and reasserts the fantasy by extending it.

The detail with which she drew the interior of the dollhouse and her mouse-eye perspective on the furnishings indicates the pleasure and persistence with which she pursued the accuracy of the drawings. She could not have clearly seen the staircase down which the mice proceed from an interior vantage point, given that there was no window in the dollhouse at that location for a photograph to be taken. Yet she could

place herself imaginatively on the staircase and draw them in anatom-
ically believable postures and in appropriate scale to the features of the
house. Her pleasure in the many realistic details of the house, which
had "real muslin curtains and a front door and a chimney" (9), led her
to strive for the inclusion of more and more miniature details in the
pictures. At one point she wrote to Norman Warne about her pleasure
in the pattern of the doll dishes included with the fake doll food: "The
little dishes are so pretty I am wondering if I have made enough of
them? Shall I squeeze in another dish?" And in the same letter she
inquired about the color of the *Encyclopedia Britannica,* which she saw
as one of the items the mice would not be able to fit in their hole.[16]
Fortunately, both the constraints of the book's format and the publisher's good advice kept her from overdoing the detail and surfeiting the
viewer.

The success both of the dollhouse and of the book lies in the myriad
details consistently miniaturized and copiously included. Potter further complicated the task for herself by using a small format, thus
miniaturizing her pictures even more. The outlines surrounding the
pictures make the details even smaller, both by the illusion of dimi-
nution that the frame creates and by limiting the picture to less than
the whole page. Her continued fascination for dollhouses and miniatures is apparent from her collection of dolls, doll clothes, and a furnished dollhouse on display at Hill Top, collections to which she added
even in her old age. Smallness for Potter was a lifetime obsession.

Part of her pleasure in telling the dollhouse story might have been
the gentle mockery she was making of the domestic arrangements in
her own home in Bolton Gardens. In another letter she wrote that the
dollhouse was "the kind of house where one cannot sit down without
upsetting something, I know the sort."[17] Though she does not say so
directly, the sterile stasis of the dolls' lives may have been modeled
after the deadening sameness with which her parents conducted their
lives. The Potters seemed unable to do anything for themselves, rely-
ing on servants to keep the house functioning. Those same servants
wrought havoc by leaving the Potters' employment or when they failed
to perform their duties exactly as the elder Potters wanted. This disruption must have seemed as devastating to the Potters as the mouse
intrusion did to the dolls. The humans increasingly expected their
daughter to oversee the servants and spare her parents the trouble of
seeing to their own household affairs. Potter's obvious pleasure in the
mice's high-spirited destruction, and her forgiveness of them in the

end, may have been an imaginative release for her and a displacement of her own desire to disturb her parents' rigidity and complacency. In any case, Potter is clearly mocking the sterility of inactive lives surrounded by functionless decoration and having a good time while she is at it.

The reader wholeheartedly applauds Potter's final disposition of the bad mice, who are not really so bad. The open ending has the other merit of accurately describing the relationship between humans and mice. Both species coexist, side by side, in perpetuity, with only occasional intrusions of the mice upon the human realm, and with subsequent intervention of the humans into mouse society, with little effect. As long as the two species do not interfere with each other, the cold war continues, if interrupted only infrequently by admiring, appreciative, and loving glimpses of the small creatures by the larger ones.

Potter identified the book as one with particular appeal to girls, and one feels her own girlish pleasure at the miniatures and the indoor views of the dollhouse and mouse hole. Her success with mice is apparent here, due most likely to their diminutive, fastidious natures, and to their willingness to become pets and to be observed. Their miniature worlds only further added to her wonder and pleasure in the fantasy world she invents for them.

The Tale of Timmy Tiptoes

By 1910 Beatrix Potter was much preoccupied with the conduct of business on her farm. Her parents, who were becoming more and more fragile in health and less able to object to their daughter's independence, still demanded what they could of her, and further distracted her from both farm and publishing. With the year 1910 began a falling off of her intense creative activity that had for the previous eight years allowed her to complete two books a year. *Timmy Tiptoes* (1911) is another squirrel story that, like *The Tale of Squirrel Nutkin*, does not call forth her best efforts. With *Timmy Tiptoes* one suspects that the problem was lack of attention and energy and a subject of American rather than British origin. Timmy is a North American gray squirrel, and his woods and neighbors, though similar to Potter's own Lake District, are not exactly the same and could not be drawn from real life. Margaret Lane suggests that Potter found the models for the animals in the

Small Mammals House of a zoo rather than in nature,[18] which may account for the animals' lack of expression.

The story is about two American gray squirrels, Timmy Tiptoes and his wife Goody, who live in an unnamed, undifferentiated wood. They differ from other gray squirrels in that they remember where they hide their nuts, and therefore have a store of great quantities. When the birds sing their natural, melodic songs, the squirrels think that they are singing, "Who's bin digging-up *my* nuts?"[19] One squirrel, who is jealous of the Tiptoe family's cache, decides that the thief that the bird refers to must be Timmy. The other squirrels gang up on Timmy and force him through a woodpecker's hole in the tree where he has been storing his nuts. He is plump, and the other squirrels squeeze him through with great effort. But once he is in, he meets a kindly chipmunk, who nurses his wounds and feeds him nuts; this treatment only makes him fatter and makes escape impossible. Goody Tiptoes searches throughout the wood for her husband and comes upon a lady chipmunk, wife of the kindly one in the tree, who complains that her husband has left her. Both find their spouses in the tree, and the chipmunk elects to move out. Timmy must wait until a storm removes the top of the tree before he can climb out and the chipmunk can move back in. From this point on, the squirrels elect to store their nuts behind a padlocked door, and no one in the woods ever again pays attention to what the birds say.

In this story, in contrast to *Squirrel Nutkin,* the squirrels are personified and wear clothing. Timmy sports a red jacket, and Goody a long pink dress. They conduct their domestic arrangements harmoniously, in contrast to the chipmunks. The lady chipmunk complains in a rhyme,

> My little old man and I fell out,
> How shall we bring this matter about?
> Bring it about as well as you can,
> And get you gone, you little old man!
>
> (41)

Like the birds' "Who's bin digging-up *my* nuts?" this rhyme explains what an animal is saying when it makes its characteristic noise. Thus, the story becomes another *pourquoi* legend, like *Squirrel Nutkin,* explaining what wild creatures say and why. But the rhyme also has other implications. Instances of domestic discord occur in other Potter books, as when Anna Maria and Samuel Whiskers argue about the proper way to make a kitten pudding. Yet the desertion of one spouse by another, the lady chipmunk's frankness about her husband's departure, and her careless attitude about whether he ever returns, are uncharacteristically abrasive and shocking in the otherwise unexceptional Miss Potter. The domestic relations between the chipmunks may accurately describe the non-monogamous mating habits of North American chipmunks, but the contrast with Goody Tiptoes' earnest quest to find her husband, and the kiss with which they greet each other when reunited, sound an unusual note in children's literature of the time, when marital disagreement was hardly ever mentioned and appeared even more infrequently in writing. Though Potter may not have meant the chipmunk marriage to be an important focus in the book, yet the chipmunks' attitudes toward each other jar the reader into a clearer focus on the union. Unfortunately, Potter did not make the squirrel marriage, in its blissful reunion, nearly as interesting as the chipmunks' nonchalant attitudes toward each other.

The book makes the reader wonder about the stability of the chipmunk family. Chippy Hackee, the husband, stays out of his home long after the situation with the squirrel demands that he do so. He returns home only when scared into it by a bear, whose presence in the wood Potter added to appeal to her North American audience, and who is otherwise superfluous to the story. The reader wonders how the lady chipmunk greeted her wandering husband, who is ill with a cold on his return. In the accompanying picture his wife looks on without expression at his bundled, shivering figure, leaving unanswered the question of what her reaction to his reappearance is. One wonders even more why, if she knows his whereabouts—"'I know where Chippy is; a little bird told me,' said Mrs. Chippy Hackee" (38)—she does not pursue him. When the squirrels return home, they are pictured in the tree limbs, tending to a new family. Potter does not posit the same happy ending for the reunion of the chipmunks, and thus begs a question of what the chipmunks will do now that they are back together. Though the squirrels are supposedly the center of the story, Potter's lack of control over the chipmunks leaves their future together ambiguous.

The choice of North American animals signals a new interest on Potter's part in her English-speaking audience beyond the British Commonwealth and her realization of the commercial possibilities in the United States. Here she deliberately chose not to write about English animals, hoping that the chipmunk and the bear, as well as the gray squirrel, would find ready acceptance with her American audience. The dedication of the book, "For Many Unknown Little Friends, Including Monica" (7), makes clear that her audience was not as clearly conceived as it was with other books which started as stories for a specific child. Perhaps this lack of a clear audience leads to the lack of imagination and control in the story, and the false step about the chipmunks' domestic relations. Monica sounds deceptively like a particular child of Potter's acquaintance, but she was simply one of many children who wrote a fan letter to Potter.

The book also marks the end of Potter's reliable, almost inexorable, output of books. Though *Mr. Tod* and *Pigling Bland* followed *Timmy,* yet they stand out as culminations rather than continuations of Potter's tradition of well-crafted, clearly imagined books. Neither the chipmunks nor the squirrels in *Timmy* are animated, either by squirrel or human expressions. Rather, all the animals look like stuffed toys dressed in dolls' clothing. Because the forest is not drawn from the country surrounding Sawrey, it has none of the infusions of warmth or character that the Sawrey woodland books have. Without an inspiration near at hand, it appears that Potter was unable to imagine her subjects clearly enough to write about and draw them.

The Tale of Johnny Town-Mouse

Beatrix Potter made one last effort to compose an original "Sawrey" book after her marriage, and turned to Aesop's fables for inspiration. *Johnny Town-Mouse* (1918) is Potter's rendition of "The City Mouse and the Town Mouse," Aesop's fable which explains why some persons prefer urban life, while others prefer rural life. She uses as her contrasts a wood mouse born in Sawrey and a mouse of the variety that invades human habitations, who lives in Hawkshead, a village about two miles distant from Sawrey. Though the choice of Hawkshead at first seems inappropriate, given that it is hardly more than a village even today, yet Potter invests it with as much commotion and urban peril as a much larger human settlement might have rendered.

The story concerns Timmie Willie, a wood mouse born in the country, who inadvertently finds himself in a hamper of vegetables being sent from farm to city manor house. Once he arrives, he is greeted by Johnny Town-Mouse, a distant cousin, who tries to pursuade him that the cat is simply a nuisance, and that its smell can be safely ignored while one sleeps in a hole in the sofa. Johnny further asserts that a diet of bacon and cake crumbs is infinitely superior to Timmy Willie's usual fare of grains. Timmy returns in the hamper after only a short visit, complaining of the noise, both of cat and of the domestic help in the house, and of the indigestible food. He invites Johnny to visit, which he does when the cat has kittens, when the mice are blamed for the death of the family canary, and when the family in the house leaves for vacation, giving the maid particular instructions to get rid of the mice during her spring cleaning. Johnny finds rural life no more to his liking than Timmie found city life, and returns by the next hamper. Potter ends by explicitly stating the moral of the story: "One place suits one person, another place suits another person." But the story does not end with the equanimity of the moral, for Potter adds one last prejudicial line: "For my part I prefer to live in the country, like Timmy Willie."[20]

In fact, the whole book prejudices Johnny Town-Mouse's case. The story is not really his, though his is the name in the title. It is really Timmie Willie's. Both Johnny and Timmy are frightened by the unfamiliar noises when they arrive for their visits, but Timmy shows an accurate perception of the situation when he takes fright: he hears the maid and the cat, both out to catch the mice. Johnny hears a cow mooing and the lawnmower running, but in spite of Timmie's explanation that the cow is dangerous only if it accidentally lies on you, the reader hardly finds this danger imminently threatening, given the quickness of mice. The lawnmower is the source of grass cuttings for a comfortable bed, and the cow gives milk; neither truly threatens the mice, and the reader concludes that Johnny is not very discriminating in his fearfulness.

Johnny complains that the country is too quiet for him, but Potter never shows the boredom of the town-mouse in the country, though she does show the confusion and bewilderment of the country mouse in the city when confronted with all the noise, most of which he is justified in fearing. The cat and the maid are ever-present menaces in the city; the man with the lawnmower appears only at a great distance in the country, and a mouse must deliberately seek out the threat of a cow. The food in the city is described, but so is the peril of gathering crumbs and jam from a dropped tea tray in the very presence of the cat, and Timmie's inability to thrive on such a diet. The menu in the country does not receive the same kind of attention, nor does Johnny's reaction to it. In fact, the city receives most of the focus in the text, while the country receives the clearest embodiment in the pictures. The lushness and the variety of vegetation in the pictures provide much of their interest, again foreshadowing the obvious prejudice that Potter maintains for the country over the city.

She further prejudices the case by not entering into the mouse-eye view of the city as thoroughly as she does in the country. In *Two Bad Mice* she had shown her ability to place herself imaginatively at mouse-eye level to the delight of the viewer, and though in *Johnny Town-Mouse* she can seat herself at the mouse dinner table, she strays from this viewpoint. At times she shows the mice from a clearly human, over-head view and the family maid at human-eye level. She does not com-mit this fault in the country pictures, where one enters the world at Timmie Willie's level, and sometimes even looks over his shoulder at the more distant prospects Potter shows. His strawberry-leaf umbrella and daisy-blossom parasol show the playful, imaginative lengths she went to in portraying country life, and the wealth of flowers that she adds to the country scenes only prejudices the reader even more in favor of Timmy Willie's way of life. The enclosed space, the mouse hole in which Timmie Willie lives, contrasted to the grandeur and vastness of Johnny Town-Mouse's palatial home further indicate Potter's prejudice for the simple, if small, country home and way of life.

The book is an unusually strident argument on the virtues of country living over city life, so strident that it seems almost a public justifi-cation for her retreat from active publication and her unwillingness to deal with the admiring public that was gradually finding its way to her door. Timmie Willie's natural animal love for the country is un-derscored by his lack of clothes throughout and his generous, if not elegant manners. The distortions that the etiquette of city life force upon the town mice is apparent from their long coattails, white ties, and address of Timmie Willie as the preposterous and pretentious "Timothy William." Potter is not nearly as evenhanded in her pre-sentation of the fable as is its original in Aesop. But given her feelings about her "unloved birthplace" in London and the demands of her pub-lishers, who were also located in London, it is small wonder that her story should be slanted the way it is.

In children's literature it is almost a truism that rural life is more salubrious and in general better for children, however vague the reasons are for this conclusion. The nostalgia for childhood and for the simple life often accompanies this conception of the rural life, located in some distant past where life was better. Potter chose to make this past her present when she moved to Sawrey. But her portrayal of the pleasures of rural life places her in the tradition of the nostalgic and reminiscent.

Appley Dapply's Nursery Rhymes and *Cecily Parsley's Nursery Rhymes*

Beatrix Potter's ability to riddle and rhyme, to take traditional nursery rhymes and rewrite them to refer to her animal characters is evident as early as *The Tailor of Gloucester* and *Squirrel Nutkin*. In fact, she so enjoyed her rhymes that she was prone to choke her stories with a surfeit of them, as with the privately printed edition of *The Tailor*.

She was inspired in her rhyme work by Randolph Caldecott, who chose for his illustrations rhymes where animals either predominated or were clearly present. These rhymes and illustrations she knew from her youth, from the original drawings her father collected, which hung in the young girl's nursery. A collection of illustrated nursey rhymes was an early favorite of hers among the projects she presented to Warne for further publication, and as early as 1902 she began preparing sketches and choosing rhymes for a book then called *Appley Dapply*. She even experimented with borders for the pictures, a curiously decorative touch that was never used with any of her books.

At the end of 1904 she presented to Norman Warne a dummy book, in a large size with ninety-four pages, containing thirty rhymes, twenty-one of which Norman Warne approved for an eventual publication. But his consistent editorial direction for Potter pointed away from such derivative, imitative work, and toward her own unique fantasies. His untimely death and the wealth of projects that occurred to Potter as she turned her attention to the farm at Sawrey pushed the project out of her mind. Her increasing inclination to invent her own stories would, no doubt, have gratified Norman Warne. Potter's obvious passion for the project, along with the excellent, painstaking work on the dummy were all recalled when the Warne company asked for another book for the 1917 publishing season. Potter declined to compose and illustrate another original story, but she suggested that the publishers return to the dummy and select the most apt and best-illustrated rhymes, to be compiled into a smaller, shorter format similar to *Miss Moppet*.

Her comparison of the project to *Miss Moppet* suggests that she conceived it as a book for very young children, with no need for them to understand longer, complicated plots. In fact, the virtue of the plan is that nursery rhymes seldom tell stories, but more commonly simply present vignettes or isolated incidents. The illustrations were some of the best, from her most careful and most creative period, and her early passion for the project was revived and gratified by the book's belated appearance. Potter suggested using other rhymes, including the story of *Cecily Parsley*, which she had made into a pamphlet as a gift for Freda Moore in 1897, for another volume to be published for 1922. The two books together do not include all of the rhymes from the original dummy version, and Potter suggested adding one new one to the first book. But the two books do include the best and most widely recognized. For example, Warne wisely left out one about dancing mushrooms, whose vegetable nature makes them inanimate and jarringly impossible to conceive as dancing. Potter's early studies of fungi had perhaps suggested the possibility to her, but her subsequent career as a teller of animal stories further suggests that vegetable stories were not even then her strong suit.

The resulting collections are short, leaving the reader wanting more from the volume, but felicitous in the choice of animals. Many of Potter's earlier creations reappear: Cecily Parsley bears an uncanny resemblance to Mrs. Rabbit, the industrious, self-supporting lady; and her gentleman callers are all familiar, especially the rabbit in the purple tailcoat smoking a pipe, who is clearly Old Mr. Bunny, later called Old Mr. Bouncer in *Mr. Tod.* The mice inhabit both old Gloucestertown and Lucinda and Jane's dollhouse, and the geese resemble Jemima Puddle-Duck and her family. Her cats, especially those who graciously cook and serve dinner in their country cottages, are Ribby and Tabitha Twitchit, and Old Mr. Pricklepin is elsewhere identified as Mrs. Tiggy-Winkle's uncle. His relationship to the laundress is underscored not only by his bright eyes, but also by his human shoes, which he grasps with characteristically wrinkled hedgehog paws. Cottontail's courtship by the black rabbit, implied in her marriage to the same as reported in *Mr. Tod,* is the subject of one rhyme, and the pigs going to market, especially along roads featuring road markers, are clearly derived from *Pigling Bland* and from the manuscript of *Pig Robinson.* The little pig serving "Gravy and potatoes" is a revised version of Pig-wig's domestic economy in the period after her marriage, though in the rhyme collection the pig is pink and Pig-wig is clearly described as a black Berkshire.

Some characters introduced for the first time include a mole, a number of guinea pigs, and Tom Tinker's dog. But the guinea pigs have a story of their own, in the yet-to-be resurrected Tupenny story of *The Fairy Caravan*, and Potter's dogs populate her Sawrey books with workmanly seriousness. Only the mole is introduced without antecedent; perhaps he was earlier inspired by the Mole in the Hans Christian Andersen story "Thumbelina." Or perhaps his origin came later, inspired by Moley in Kenneth Grahame's *The Wind in The Willows*. In any case, the form of the mole rhyme, a limerick, seems more clearly derived from Edward Lear. Potter's "Diggory Delvet," along with the rhyme about the "Amiable Guinea-pig," are rare instances of limericks written for children by someone other than Lear.

Occasionally, the rhymes are clearly traditional and not Potter's. "Three Blind Mice," "Tom Tinker's Dog," "Goosey Gander," and "This Little Pig Went to Market" are cases in point. The charming and successful quality of the pictures and the originality of the rhymes, either as they were rewritten by Potter or reinterpreted by her pictures, inspire in the reader a desire for more such rhymes. As individual vignettes, they do not interrupt longer stories, where early in her career Potter was inclined to insert them without much judgment as to their diversion of the story line. The larger format originally proposed for *Appley Dapply* would have better suited some of the illustrations, where detail is obscured by the reduction of the original drawings. Though the publishers' and Potter's wish to trade on the popularity and recognition of Potter books in the standard size is understandable, yet one could wish that the original dummy could be reproduced as she planned in the larger format, with the scrollwork Potter had designed to frame the drawings.

The Tale of Little Pig Robinson

Though this is the last of the books to be published in the Peter Rabbit series, *Little Pig Robinson* was inspired by an early vacation that the Potters took when Beatrix was seventeen. She began to compose the story as early as 1893. In 1901 and 1902 she again turned to the story and revised it, and in 1929, when she was importuned by Warne and by her American publisher, David McKay, for a book for both houses to publish simultaneously, she brought out her manuscript yet once more.

The story of the little pig concerns his being sent to market by his aunts, who are too rotund to make the journey themselves, and their commissions for him to perform while at the market. In his naiveté

about the world he is abducted by a sailor and impressed into a ship's
gang, not so much to work as to grow fat and provide a splendid meal.
When the ship's cat lets Little Pig know of the cook's intention, the
two animals design an escape for the pig, who successfully steers himself "to the land where the Bong Tree grows—," where he establishes
himself as the pig with a ring in his nose who becomes a permanent
resident there and who greets the arrival of the owl and the pussycat
from the poem by Edward Lear.

At this point in her career Potter was still capable of turning the
terse, ironic phrase. But *Pig Robinson* is not one of her last works, but
one of her earliest, resurrected to satisfy her publisher and little revised
for the purpose. For example, Potter describes the fates of Robinson's
aunts thus: "They led prosperous uneventful lives, and their end was
bacon."[21] Though the comment has much of the acerbity of her best
books, the tone of voice and attitude of dry social criticism do not
prevail throughout the book. But many of the incidents on the farm
and on the road to market are derived from *Pigling Bland,* where another little pig had been sent to market according to the old nursery
rhyme. The seaside market scene contains much of the activity and
color that one expects from Potter's close observations of humans and
animals. But the narrative of Robinson's life on board the ship is pe-
culiarly shortened, especially for a book that promises in its title to
send him on remarkable adventures, and ends just as he arrives in the
land of the Bong Tree. The opening chapter, describing the port but
not clearly relating it to Robinson's fate, seems out of place and filled
with an uncharacteristic nostalgia for a past vacation emanating from
the writer herself and not from the story. The pictures of the little pig
in the marketplace, many of which were cut from the English version
now available in the Peter Rabbit series, but formerly available in the
McKay edition, are some of her best. But the realism with which she
shows the market scene contrasts jarringly with the fantasy picture of
the land of the Bong Tree, festooned with its childlike fantasy of
sweets. The tropical paradise was beyond Potter's grasp; in fact, in *Pig
Robinson* the scenes that succeed are those set on land.

The book is the longest of the Peter Rabbit series, and its sparsity
of illustration, combined with its copious text, place it more properly
among her American books of her later period. Though Potter was still
capable of an occasional elegantly turned phrase, the longer text did
not provide her with enough concentration on the individual words,
and the story is long without needing to be so. The pictures, that in

the past had provided a kind of discipline for her writing, keeping her from going on too long and concentrating her more clearly on her writing, are not numerous enough in this book to keep the style from flabbiness and unnecessary description. Though the imagination that could take a children's traditional nursery rhyme for inspiration and spin an independent story from it is still evident, yet the story is less satisfactory and taut than the best of her writing, and the narrative is not honed with that intensity that drove her to perfect her earlier work.

At this point Potter had not written anything new for Warne since 1918 and *Johnny Town-Mouse.* She had supplied a few books to David McKay, ostensibly because she considered that her American audiences were more appreciative of her work. But it would seem that secretly, she knew that these works were not her best, and she did not want them judged by the perceptive eyes of her own country. She was in the process of raising money for her endeavors with the National Trust, and was not particular about how she made this money, for her writing had become less important to her than her efforts to preserve her countryside. The stories of this "American period" were tossed off easily, with little rewriting and little of the concentrated intensity of the drawings of her earlier books. Instead, she relied on quick pen-and-ink sketches, usually in larger format than the Peter Rabbit books, that would tax neither her eyesight nor her time.

By contrast with her more productive period, one finds a writer more involved with fairy tales and romance than with the hard, difficult truths of life that she portrayed in the earlier books. One also finds a writer from whom the public craved work and from whom they would accept anything with pleasure. So she felt less inclined to rework her material and less amenable to editorial suggestion, now that it was the publishers who wanted her, instead of her being dependent on the publishers. These "American" books, with the exception of *Little Pig Robinson,* are not included in the Peter Rabbit series for reasons other than their length: they are not true to the spirit of the earlier books, and they are not as well executed.

Though Potter never wished to pander to her audience and always maintained that she wrote to please herself, the importunities of her reading public for more books when she was no longer interested in writing them led her to fantasize stories set in fairy-tale realms rather than to create them from the reality surrounding her. The tiredness of her writing is evident, as is her desire to satisfy the public's demand for more books and her own requirements for more money. She felt that her public would be pleased with stories they might not have found satisfactory had the writer been anyone else. Her fame was now great enough to support the sales of less-than-satisfactory books, even in Britain. Potter always maintained that she could not write to order; but the continued need for more money and the demands for more books placed a kind of order upon her for more work, whatever the quality. The results of these requests for more are not as felicitous as her earlier creations. Her ability to cast a magic spell, never as strong as her ability to weave a tale based on reality, got her what she wanted: the continued adulation of her public and more money, though not the critical acclaim for these later books that the earlier ones have gained.

Chapter Four
The Sawrey Books

The purchase of Hill Top Farm in 1905 signaled a change in Beatrix Potter's writing and an explosion of her creative energy. Norman Warne's death in the same summer left her without the editorial guidance that had shaped her books to that point, but the loss of both editor and fiancé did not mean the end of her career. Warne's influence had so shaped her literary and artistic styles that she now saw herself as sole arbiter of good writing and drawing. With this self-confidence came the motivation and perseverance to embark on a new kind of book, about the country and village around her, with more complicated, sometimes sinister plots and a greater variety of animals. The skill with which she both narrated and illustrated grew, as did her daring with story construction, especially as the stories revolve around more and more ominous villains.

Roger Sale locates the liberation of this energy in the reassurance Potter felt in the ownership of her own home.[1] As her animal characters sought small, snug homes, so did their creator. Once she found a space of her own to decorate and order as she saw fit, with no interference from her parents or restrictive social customs, she relaxed enough to let loose the creative energies that were held in check, if only barely, in London. The attention she lavished on her farm and home in refurbishing them was echoed in the attention she paid them in her books of this period. Though the earliest of the so-called Sawrey books place animals in their natural habitats, in the countryside around the village of Near Sawrey, as soon as she acquired the house, she set about cataloging the details of its decor, in the books about cats. And even though the earliest Sawrey books do not take place on Hill Top Farm or in the village, yet she rewrote both *Mrs. Tiggy-Winkle* and *Jeremy Fisher* completely before publishing them, to make their characters and landscape consistent with the Lake District countryside. Though Potter and Norman Warne had a number of projects in various stages that they were considering for publication, yet Potter never looked back to them until she was past this remarkably productive period. The life she found around her in her own home was sufficiently rich in inspiration to provide all the story material she needed.

The Tale of Mrs. Tiggy-Winkle

Of all her animal creations Mrs. Tiggy-Winkle is one of Potter's most novel, for it is seldom that one sees in literature a personified hedgehog. Though animals of the unconventional, unpettable sort do occasionally appear in fairy tales and other children's stories, yet, with the exception of Kenneth Graham's riverbank characters, such animals are not usually well-developed or frequent actors in the stories. On the other hand, Mrs. Tiggy-Winkle is Potter's unique re-creation of the stodginess of a hedgehog into a fastidious washerwoman. The story is reminiscent of *Alice in Wonderland* in the dream-vision that Potter suggests to explain Lucie's visit to the hedgehog's home. But Mrs. Tiggy is created so consistently and convincingly as a country washerwoman that the reader hardly believes that Lucie, the little girl to whom Mrs. Tiggy appears, was only dreaming.

Potter originally wrote Mrs. Tiggy's story for a young cousin of hers, Stephanie Hyde-Parker. But while she was doing the sketches on her 1901 vacation in the Lake District, she made friends with Lucie Carr, the daughter of the vicar of Newlands, near Keswick. Lucie's baby talk—evident in the book in her mispronunciation of the words "pinafore" and "handkerchief"—and her blonde hair made her an attractive model for Lucie in the book, and so the story became hers when Potter published it in 1905. *The Tale of Jeremy Fisher,* published the following year, became Stephanie's book when Potter dedicated it to her.

The story concerns Lucie's forgetful habit of losing her pocket handkerchiefs and pinafores during play. While she is out looking for them, she finds Mrs. Tiggy-Winkle's neat cottage and her carefully kept kitchen. Mrs. Tiggy is a "clear-starcher,"[2] a variety of laundress whose expertise lies in the preparation of those smaller articles of clothing—frills, shirtfronts, collars, and cuffs—without which no proper Victorian person could consider himself or herself well dressed. She not only launders clothes, she irons and starches them as well. Modern electric irons have taken much of the drudgery out of the task. But one has only to remember the delicacy with which natural fabrics, elegantly frilled, tucked, and pleated, must be treated to imagine Mrs. Tiggy's skill and to understand her pride in her work. That the modern electric iron has replaced the cast-iron flatiron which was unevenly heated over a wood fire further indicates her skillfulness in her craft.

Given that Victorian dressing was such an elaborate affair, with voluminous skirts, petticoats, trousers, and ties, a successful laundress had many garments from many different patrons to keep track of. Remembering her patrons' preferences in starching and styling would have proven a formidable enterprise. Mrs. Tiggy-Winkle is a representative of the successful members of her profession. She has many clients, including animals from earlier Potter books. Lucie wonders at Mrs. Tiggy's brown face and wrinkled hands, all of which could be explained by her frequent journeys out-of-doors and her habitual submersion of hands in water. The many hairpins protruding from her clothes, "sticking wrong end out" (46) keep Lucie at a distance, but altogether the visit is successful. Lucie relocates her handkerchiefs and pinafore among Mrs. Tiggy's unmarked laundry and shares a hospitable cup of tea with the laundress.

When Lucie leaves and turns around to thank her hostess, she finds Mrs. Tiggy scampering off with none of her washerwoman's garb, and revealing her true identity as a hedgehog. Potter raises the question in the final paragraph as to whether the story is true, but the narrator's authoritative voice intrudes to point out the inconsistency of Lucie's sleeping through her own retrieval of her clothes. The narrator further documents the reality of Mrs. Tiggy's existence by pointing out her own acquaintance with Mrs. Tiggy and her home.

The story was written from Potter's own intimate familiarity with and affection for a pet hedgehog, acquired on one of the family vacations. The eyes of this particular pet engaged Potter's fancy, and there are many sketches of hedgehogs personified in Potter's early work, before she went on to become a published author-illustrator. Mrs. Tiggy's chattiness and competence derive from her model, a Kitty Macdonald, washerwoman to the Potter family during their summer vacations in Scotland from 1871 to 1882. Potter visited this woman several times after the family had decided to spend their holidays elsewhere, and was particularly struck by the woman's lively, active intelligence and phenomenal memory, even at the advanced age of eighty-four. The suitability of the hedgehog as personifier of the washerwoman arose out of their mutual rotundity and affection for the author. As a longtime friend and traveling companion of the author, Mrs. Tiggy presented herself as a likely candidate for a book of her own as early as 1901.

While Mrs. Tiggy's quizzical, perceptive eye and felicitous reincarnation as a washerwoman are part of the book's success, the drawings of Lucie are one of its chief failures. Potter had trouble drawing the little girl, not because the model was unwilling to pose, but because, once again, she was faced with her own inability to draw humans. The drawings of Lucie were further complicated by Potter's lack of attention to one significant detail: the color of Lucie's cloak, red in some of the original drawings, blue in others, and soft brown in her revisions. When she saw the first proofs of the pictures, she was indecisive about the red or blue, but both colors appeared too hot and vivid for Mrs. Tiggy's muted, pastel world. Both author and editor decided on brown for the final pictures. Potter drew and redrew Lucie's figure, both because of the editor's demand for better pictures, and because of the obvious need for consistency in the color of Lucie's cloak. Lucie's features were rubbed out and drawn again, sometimes even cut out and pasted in again on the original drawings as Potter worked through her revisions. As a result, the final pictures of Lucie are blurred, with none of the bold, sure line that Potter confidently used to draw Mrs. Tiggy. The little girl's postures were awkward and stiff and compare unfavorably to Mrs. Tiggy's deft, bustling activity in her kitchen. Potter tried recomposing some of the pictures to minimize her problems with the little girl's figure, exchanging Mrs. Tiggy's full back view for Lucie's, but nothing seems to have succeeded. Lucie in some pose or other, however minimized her presence might be in the picture, still had to appear.

The plot is also thin, with little of the complication evident in the earlier *Two Bad Mice* or later Sawrey books. It is Mrs. Tiggy's personality and lifestyle that hold the book together. Potter admitted to Norman Warne that she thought the book was another one for girls, like *Two Bad Mice,* and that girls would find the clothing particularly interesting.[3] Like *Two Bad Mice, Mrs. Tiggy-Winkle* is also a story that revolves around a house, this time a hedgehog's burrow. Like most girls' books, the scene is primarily interior and the interests domestic. But there is a significant change from the mouse book to the hedgehog book in regard to domestic arrangements: Mrs. Tiggy is a countrywoman, and the detail of the stone floors, open hearth, and simple but comfortable bench before the fire, all show Potter's approval of the hedgehog's simple but cozy household. There is none of the ironic commentary about human housekeeping that the reader finds in *Two Bad Mice.* Instead, the reader finds total, loving approbation of the laundress, her home, and her pride in her business. One suspects that

Potter found in Mrs. Tiggy many of the virtues she sought to pursue in her own life as a farmer and homeowner.

Though the scene is primarily interior, *Mrs. Tiggy-Winkle* gives the first glimpses of Potter's rural countryside, which she portrayed more fully as her Sawrey books progressed. There are a few wide vistas, showing the mountains which later connoted permanence and reliability for the author. There are stone fences, country pathways, and homes of natural, unadorned materials. *Mrs. Tiggy-Winkle* is the first of the books to celebrate this simple, unchanging way of life, and Potter's admiration for it is evident.

Potter was developing a clear sense of how to market her books, and, by bringing in the laundry of her earlier characters, she recalls them to her readers and helps to create a continuity between them and Mrs. Tiggy's universe. Peter Rabbit and Benjamin Bunny reappear to collect the slightly shrunken blue coat and red bandana handerchief, smelling reminiscently of onions, of the earlier rabbit stories. Squirrel Nutkin has sent a tailcoat with no tail, recalling his notorious end, or lack thereof, in his story. Other characters, familiar from nursery rhymes and children's stories, also send laundry: Sally Henny-Penny sends stockings, badly worn in the heel from her scratching in the farmyard, and Tom Titmouse, a dicky bird in common parlance, sends dicky shirt fronts. Cock Robin, though he sends no laundry, also appears in the book as a possible source of information as to the whereabouts of Lucie's lost garments. Potter's world was becoming increasingly populous, and she made use of her former creations to give a sense of consistency and reality to her animal worlds, both for inner consistency within each book, and for consistency among them all. Mrs. Tiggy reappears in *Ginger and Pickles* as a purchaser of soap, and thus lends credibility to the mercantile practices of the dog and cat shopkeepers.

Though at the end Potter does address the reader in her own tone of voice, thereby taking a chance with breaking the objective tone of the narrator, her authorial intrusion in the end is limited to one paragraph on the last page, set in smaller type than the rest of the text. Her pointing to the inconsistency of Lucie finding her handkerchiefs and lost pinafore while asleep underscores the inner consistency of the whole story. But the fervor, complete with italics, with which she declares, "And besides—*I* have seen that door into the back of the hill called Cat Bells—and besides *I* am very well acquainted with dear Mrs. Tiggy-winkle!" (59) emphasizes in a tone simultaneously childlike and adult the reality of Lucie's experience. The certainty and emphasis with which she underlines her "I" asserts the adult authority, while the repetition of the "and besides" mirrors a child's way of building up emphasis, by parallel coordinate constructions and repetitions. The conclusion, that Mrs. Tiggy is real and so is Lucie's dream, appears inevitable.

Potter's mentions of the lambs' coats from the various small towns around Lucie's home at Newlands give the stories both local color and conviction, for they locate Lucie's story in a real place. At the same time, the town names may not be familiar to children unacquainted with British geography, or simply too young to know such details. Skelghyl and Gatesgarth, like Little-town, may be construed by an inexperienced reader as places and names of genuine Anglo-Saxon antiquity. Their inclusion in the story both localizes it and mythologizes it in some remote past before mechanical means of doing laundry existed, when washerwomen might really have been hedgehogs. Though Mrs. Tiggy is not the usual variety of animal found in beast stories, yet her name has become synonymous with lady hedgehogs and fastidious housekeepers.

The Pie and the Patty-Pan

Potter composed both *The Tale of Tom Kitten* and *The Pie and the Patty-Pan* during the first year after she bought Hill Top Farm. She had earlier had an idea for a story about a dog and a cat at a tea party, and had gone as far as to compose the story in an exercise book and block out sketches for it for her editor to preview. However, the story was not pursued and was laid aside for the time, while she and Norman Warne prepared *The Tale of Squirrel Nutkin* for publication for 1903. After Norman's death in 1905 Potter bought Hill Top and went back to the story, to revise it totally, using an attractive Pomeranian living in Sawrey as the model for her dog, one of the cats at Hill Top for her cat, and her own farmhouse and the surrounding village of Near Sawrey for her setting. Part of her motivation for picking up the old story and revising it was the obvious pleasure she found in drawing her own house. A few of the street scenes were drawn at Hawkshead, a larger village near Sawrey, but the rest of the pictures show scenes that are still visible in Near Sawrey and at Hill Top today.

The story concerns the very proper social relations between the Pomeranian, named Duchess, and her neighbor cat, Mrs. Ribston Pippin, nicknamed Ribby. Ribby, the fictional mistress of Potter's cottage at Hill Top, invites her friend Duchess to tea, using as her medium of communication the local mail service. In her letter she even goes so far as to describe the menu, which will be pie, and urges Ribby to be on time, for the pie is all for the guest while the hostess will content herself with muffins. Duchess is pleased to accept, again by mail, but is concerned about the contents of the pie, which will be, more likely than not, mouse. The guest is not as convinced as the hostess that the repast will be *"most delicious,"*[4] though she edits her concern out of her reply and assures her hostess that the pie will be "fine" (11).

Part of Ribby's persuasion in her letter includes a description of the serving dish as "a pie-dish with a pink rim" (7-8). Duchess has a matching pie-dish and resolves to substitute her ham-and-veal pie into Ribby's oven on the day of the party, while the hostess is not looking. The plan would have worked well, if only Duchess had known that Ribby bakes pies in the lower part of the oven, while Duchess puts her pie in the upper part. Furthermore, Ribby's pie has no tin patty-pan in it to help it keep its shape, while Duchess's pie does have such a device. When Duchess finally arrives for the party, she eats the pie Ribby serves, thinking it is her own. But Duchess is concerned at the end of the meal that the patty-pan which she had used in her own pastry is gone, and that she has eaten it. Panic-stricken, she sends Ribby for the doctor, in this animal town a magpie and a supposed expert on pies.

While the hostess is gone, Duchess investigates the top door of the oven, only to find her own pie with the patty-pan still cooking there. Relieved to find that she has not swallowed the patty-pan whole, she discreetly places the pie and pie-dish outside the backdoor, to be retrieved when Ribby will not be watching. Though the idea of eating mouse still upsets her stomach, Ribby and the doctor return to find Duchess much improved and ready to return home to recuperate. But the doctor-magpie beats Duchess to the backyard and consumes her pie with friends, breaking the dish and revealing the patty-pan in the process. In the morning Ribby is surprised to find both the patty-pan and the broken pie-dish in her yard, and cannot figure out just how her dish could come to be broken and her patty-pan misplaced when both are stored in her kitchen.

The story focuses on the social relations between neighbors in a small town. The overly formal quality of the etiquette being observed is clear from the letters Ribby and Duchess use to communicate with each

other, when a short trip down the road by either party could have just
as easily delivered the same messages. The care with which Duchess
composes the letter of response, changing "I hope it isn't mouse?" to
"I hope it will be fine," (11) in order to avoid offending her friend
shows the extremes to which friends could go to avoid the slightest
note of controversy. Of couse, it is also clear that Ribby is not being a
considerate hostess, serving what she would consider appetizing, but
not considering her friend's tastes and preferences. Still, Ribby is well-
intentioned, as is clear by her generosity in offering Duchess the whole
pie to herself, and certainly a friend's feelings should be spared, though
the lengths to which one might have to go to do so might be ques-
tioned here.

The stiffness of their relations is again underscored by the two animals passing each other, Ribby on her way to market, Duchess on her
way to substitute the pies, without speaking to each other "because
they were going to have a party" (27). Potter's explanation tells as
much about the animals' behavior as does their own rationalization
about having the party as mannerly motivation for avoiding each other.
It is clear that the two do not speak to each other for reasons more
significant than that they will be seeing each other soon anyhow. Duchess does not want to reveal her plan to switch pies. Ribby's reasons are
less clear, but perhaps she does not speak because she is being extremely polite or because she is extremely rushed. Duchess's anxiety to arrive
on time and yet not to arrive early causes her to rush out of the house
and then to wait outside Ribby's house before knocking. Her "most
genteel little tap-tappity" at Ribby's door and her inquiry of Ribby,
who is standing right in front of her guest, "Is Mrs. Ribston at home?"
(42), which she clearly is, all underscore the elaborate code of behavior
practiced not only by the animals, but also, by extension, the villagers
of Near Sawrey. In Potter's eyes, the result of so much etiquette was
nonsensical, distorted behavior. Yet the animals remain friends at the
end of the story, and because of their careful avoidance of offense, the
social pretense and elaborate code of etiquette are maintained.

Duchess's misapprehension about her own swallowing of the patty-
pan points to the naiveté not only of the animals, but also of Potter's
neighbors. Duchess and Ribby are clearly animals and were not modeled after any particular villagers. None of Potter's fellow townspeople
ever took offense at her inclusion of the town in her books. But perhaps
their lack of reaction is a further indication of their naiveté about her
purpose of pointing out human foibles in her books. Both Ribby and

Duchess panic over the unlikely possibility that Duchess has swallowed the patty-pan, just as her neighbors must have panicked over unlikelihoods that Potter considered laughable. Duchess makes herself sick at the thought, even though she has just eaten a mouse pie, which she had previously thought would have made her even more ill. In fact, she likes the mouse pie.

Her illness is just a case of nerves, maybe even of hypochondria. And yet neither Ribby nor Duchess herself confront the little dog with the fact that she could not possibly have eaten the patty-pan, or at least could not have done so without noticing. Duchess never truly admits that she thoroughly enjoys eating mouse pie. In fact, no one in the story admits anything. At the end, with no suspicions or information, Ribby is left with the mystery of the patty-pan and the broken pie-dish, which she in her ignorance cannot figure out for herself.

Potter's focus in the story was as much on the picturesque beauty of the village as on the elaborate, if humorous, mannerliness of her neighbors. In a pattern that she was to repeat in later Sawrey books she lavished as much attention on the details of the floral profusion in the village and in her own garden as on the story itself. In fact, the story is a rather confusing one, and not one of her most popular, perhaps because it depends on a knowledge of old stoves used in open fireplaces and a series of inferences about the two pies that may be hard for very young children to figure out.

And yet the pictures are some of the most beautiful she ever drew, especially those of the many doorways and garden plots, with flowers typical of the various locales. The colors here are not the usual muted greens and browns that the viewer has come to expect of Potter, nor of the simple contrasts resulting from the colors of individual animals' clothing, with muted reds and blues chosen for their values of contrast. Rather, Potter used the whole range of bright colors, including oranges, violets, and bright yellows seldom seen in her other books. Even Ribby's carefully chosen lilac silk dress shows Potter's concern for color, and Duchess's luxurious black mane is unusually decorative for Potter's dogs.

The details of her house, including the oven with three doors, the top being decorative and unfunctional, as the narrative specifies, and the coronation teapot that Ribby proudly uses for this state occasion, are lovingly and minutely detailed. Potter even specifies that the hearthrug is made of rabbit pelts (in Potter's own house, the rug was of lambskin), and even the kinds of plants she had inside her house,

which are all carefully and colorfully detailed, with much more bright-
ness than in other Potter books. The large format that Warne used to
issue the book originally, the captions under each picture, and the
occasional lack of coordination between text and illustration, show her
delight in the pictures, sometimes at the expense of the text. And yet
her pride of ownership is evident, and one suspects that even if she had
to observe manners as peculiar as those of Ribby and Duchess, yet
Potter would have done so to make herself part of the village and es-
tablish herself as a hostess and accomplished homemaker.

The Tale of Mr. Jeremy Fisher

Soon after she wrote to Noel Moore about Peter Rabbit's story in
1893, Potter wrote another picture letter to his younger brother Eric
about the adventures of a frog who goes fishing. The scene was set on
the River Tay near one of the Potters' Scottish vacation sites where Mr.
Potter and his friends frequently fished. This character appears to have
been as memorable for Beatrix Potter as was Peter Rabbit, for as early
as 1902 she suggested making the story of Jeremy Fisher the frog into
a book. In 1894 she had published a short pamphlet with Ernest Nister, about a frog who also went fishing. For want of time, she put aside
the frog book for the Warne company in favor of other projects. But
when she became enamored of life in Sawrey, she took up the frog book
again, this time transforming him into a resident of the pond in the
south of the Lake District. She bought the plates and copyright back
from Ernest Nister and proceeded to write and illustrate the story of
Jeremy Fisher.

In length and simplicity the story is geared for an audience of about
the same age as *Peter Rabbit*. Like *Peter Rabbit*, the story is set in some
obscure past, though it can be more definitely located by Jeremy Fisher's wardrobe of a Regency-period dandy. Jeremy, like a leisured, land-
ed gentleman, decides one day to go fishing for sport. His plans
include catching enough fish to invite friends over to share the catch.
He sets out, but is beset by bad luck, including a water beetle who
pinches his toe, the catch of a stickleback who is too big and too prick-
ly for the frog to handle, and being swallowed by a trout, who lets
him go, owing to the bad taste of his fishing jacket. He vows never to
go fishing again, and invites his friends to join him for a dinner where
the menu includes only delicacies available on land.

Potter had long been familiar with frogs, both as pets and as specimens. The choice of the Regency costume for the amphibian is particularly felicitous, given the attention that Regency dress focuses on dainty feet and the tight-fitting trousers that show off footwear. Jeremy Fisher's thin legs are humanized by his galoshes and pumps. In fact, his feet are the most expressive part of his body, for they indicate his leisurely attitude toward life, as when he elegantly props them up above his head or casually crosses them in front of him. His upright posture seems perfectly consistent both with frog and human, and yet, when the trout captures him and eats his galoshes, he is pictured swimming away with toes splayed and the froggy webbing between them visible. Potter uses the hump on his back to define the humanness of his postures in intense concentration and effort, while still clearly denoting his basic form as a frog. In combining both frog and dandy, she made best use of both aspects to define her character as both leisurely human and instinctive frog.

She is equally felicitous in her choice of the newt and the tortoise as the friends of Jeremy Fisher, for their postures also lend themselves to characterizations as English country gentlemen of leisure. Ptolemy Tortoise, the alderman, is a large, hulking figure with an immense shell resembling a heavy overcoat. The chain and medallion of office around his neck befits his stature of the elder statesman of the pond. His preference for vegetarian fare, consistent not only with his nature as a tortoise but also with his character of English eccentric, leads him to carry a string bag of salad with him, again consistent with his character of elegant, generous guest and yet finicky eater. Sir Isaac Newton's name is obviously chosen for its suggestiveness about his newt species. But the creation of an elegant waistcoat out of the mottled coloring of the local newts and the addition of the bulky Regency necktie suggest as much about his humanness as about his species. The necktie makes his neck long, which is consistent with both Regency costume and newt skeletal structure, while the tailcoat is the only appropriate garb for an animal-human with a tail.

This book is one of the few Potter books in which female characters are not included, and the activities presented in it are consistent not only with males-only entertainments but also with the natures of these pond inhabitants. Jeremy Fisher goes boating, using his own personal lilypad, but propels himself by poling or punting, a typical leisure activity for Regency gentlemen and those of Potter's own time. Jeremy is heavily equipped for fishing, as though he cultivates it more as an intensely interesting sport and hobby than a livelihood. He has adven-

tures, which he relates to his friends in animated tones when they come
to dinner. And the dinner itself is not just a casual repast or simple
tea. It is a large-scale production, with an elegantly served main course
of roasted grasshopper, displayed in all its glory on a platter, comple-
mented by ladybird sauce. The elaborate detail and copious quantities
of the provisions all indicate the passion with which elegant cuisine is
pursued among the leisured gentlemen.

One cannot help but suspect that Potter modeled these gentlemanly
activities after those of her father and his friends at his club. Their sole
concern in life was how to occupy their leisure time, and the activities
they invented to do so were pursued sometimes to the point of absurd
obsession. They did little that was useful or needful, but yet they con-
trived to enjoy themselves. As Potter conceived of it, life on the edge
of the pond was equally leisurely, though life-and-death concerns occasionally surfaced, as when Jeremy is swallowed but not digested by
the trout. But usually one had simply to be careful in order to avoid
such circumstances, though the risk might occasionally be worth the
extravagant story one could tell about one's adventures when the incident was all over.

In *Jeremy Fisher* Potter celebrated and preserved the leisurely lives
and characters of her aquatic acquaintances in the country she was
growing to love. As much as she found the lives of her father and his
male acquaintances humorous and trivial, yet she valued their outdoor
pursuits and the pleasure they found in nature, it would seem from her
use of their sports in this book. She valued nature untouched by humans even more, as is clear from the careful observation she shows in
her pictures. The story is not a particularly complicated one and was
apparently written with few of her usually relentless revisions. Yet the
pictures have a finished quality without this effort. They are truly remarkable in their coloring, dominated by the blue water and green
marine growth. Her ability to show human society without also implying its damaging effects on flora and fauna further underscores the
book's felicitous composition and success.

The Tale of Tom Kitten

Tom Kitten is the first of Beatrix Potter's Sawrey books and introduces
characters that she used in nearly all of the books about Sawrey that
followed. Though one usually thinks of cats as pets, on a farm they are
working animals and must earn their keep. Though they fall into the

category of what Potter elsewhere called "serious" animals,[5] yet they are also full of character and mischief. Tabitha Twitchit was a longtime feline resident of the farm at Hill Top, and an important ally in the perennial battle against the rats who threatened the conduct of businesslike farming. It is not surprising, then, to find her a focal character in three of Potter's books, and a peripheral character in one other. Her character here is a blend of Potter herself and someone who probably resembled Potter's mother, or perhaps some other proper Victorian matron.

Tom Kitten is a book about manners and how children react to them. The story was inspired not only by the real Tabitha Twitchit, but also by a friend's kitten that Potter borrowed for her sketches for the book. Kittens are by nature playful, but Tom, like Peter Rabbit, is unusually defiant of parental prohibitions. When Tabitha, mother of kittens named Mittens, Tom Kitten, and Moppet, expects some other lady cats for tea, she carefully grooms and dresses her children, and then sends them out of her way, with specific prohibitions against becoming untidy. Let loose in the garden, the kittens do exactly what their mother has forbidden, first soiling their clothes and then losing them to a family of ducks, who retrieve them as the kittens gradually discard them. When their mother finds her offspring, her sense of social propriety is mortified, and she sends them upstairs to bed. She misrepresents to her guests that the children have the measles, while the guests in turn try to ignore the sounds of the kittens' romp in the bedroom. Meanwhile, the ducks wear the kittens' clothing while swimming and lose the garments at the bottom of the pond, where they look for them still. Thus, Potter explains in the fashion of the *pourquoi* fairy tale why ducks are so frequently seen with their heads in the water and their tails upright: they are looking for the clothes they have stolen from Tom Kitten and his sisters.

One suspects that the opening line of the story was inspired by the nursery rhyme about the three little kittens who lost their mittens, and their mother's consequent punishment of denying them their dinner. It certainly seems likely that the name Mittens comes from the rhyme, and Moppet from *The Story of Miss Moppet,* the book for the very young child that Potter was planning at this time. In her book Miss Moppet is another blue-eyed tiger kitten, like this trio, and her potential for a story is hardly explored in depth in her short vignette. Tom Kitten, elsewhere addressed by his mother as Thomas, is a name similar to Tomcat, Peter Rabbit, or Benjamin Bunny—a combination of a formal, human first name with an animal last name. The name Tom is also suggestive of a kind of carefree, rugged outdoor boyishness. In fact, the three Toms of children's literature—Tom Sawyer, Tom Brown, and Tom Aldrich—define that nineteenth-century variety of active, mischievous boyhood that children's literature perpetuates and that Potter here uses to define her naughty-boy kitten. The transformation of Tom into Thomas is managed by his mother's attempt to dignify the rascal kitten, both by her calling forth of the dignity of his full name and by her attempt to dress him in "all sorts of elegant uncomfortable clothes"[6] which make the kitten look like a cross between little Lord Fauntleroy and Tom Sawyer on his way to church.

Of course, Tabitha's attempt succeeds no better than Mrs. Rabbit's, when she takes Peter firmly by the collar and buttons the top of his blue jacket. Both mothers issue their taboos, which their sons, in particular, ignore. But in the case of Mrs. Rabbit there is a rational reason for her dictum. She clearly explains her reasons to her children, and the rule is for their own good. Tabitha simply lists things and people for the children to avoid, with no reasons given, though most readers will be able to infer the motives behind her list: "Now keep your frocks clean, children! You must walk on your hind legs. Keep away from the dirty ash-pit, and from Sally Henny Penny, and from the pig-stye and the Puddle-Ducks" (22). Not only has the mother forced the kittens into unnatural human clothes, she forces them into unnatural human postures.

But keeping their clothes clean is only possible if the kittens stand erect; when they fall, their clothes become grass-stained and disheveled. The prohibitions against the ash-pit and the pig-stye are clear, for these are sources of dirt. The name Puddle-Ducks suggests a watery source of besmirching. It is not entirely clear why the kittens may not go to see Sally Henny Penny, but there are a number of explanations that would make sense of this dictum: cats and hens usually do not coexist peacefully. Perhaps the hen would lead the kittens into situations where they would get dirty. Perhaps the hen is simply being snubbed by Tabitha. In any case, she is part of a rather complicated list of pitfalls for the kittens to avoid, and it is no wonder that the kittens disobey. As Potter herself says, "Mrs. Tabitha unwisely turned them out into the garden, to be out of the way . . ." (22). She places the kittens in the path of temptation and then muddles, rather than clarifies the situation with her lengthy injunction.

Like Peter Rabbit, Tom Kitten gets into trouble when he ascends the garden wall. Unlike Peter, Tom's loss of his clothes is not a great tragedy to him, but rather a blessing. Potter makes clear from the beginning that the kittens do not appreciate or sympathize with their mother's attempts to impress her friends. They put up with having their faces washed and their fur brushed. But when Tabitha combs their tails and whiskers, Tom fights back by scratching, a sensible reaction to all the intrusive fussiness that the kittens have endured thus far. Given that combing, which tugs more painfully at the hairs than brushing, is the most invasive manipulation that their mother has perpetrated on them, the reader sympathizes with his attempts to fight back. Tom is thus defined by his scratching as both "very naughty" (17) and very sensible.

Tabitha futher attempts to transform him by putting him in fussy clothes that restrict his movement and by insisting that the too-small clothes stay buttoned, in spite of the propensity of the buttons to burst off because of Tom's plumpness. But these actions are no more successful than the washing and brushing. While Peter Rabbit's clothing defines his personhood, Tom Kitten's clothing perverts and distorts his unconforming animal nature. The inevitability of his final liberation from the blue suit, in spite of his sisters' attempts to redress him and refasten buttons which have previously burst off, is a liberation of his true kitten self. Mittens and Moppet try to deal with their pinafores and tuckers by turning them around, and wearing them backwards, so that the encumbering fabric is at their backs and no longer hampers their movement on all fours. But Tom's suit is particularly torturous, for it prevents him from doing what his sisters do. He can barely walk on his hind legs, and he certainly cannot follow them up the wall to sit with them at the top.

When he finally reaches the top, "He was all in pieces" and his sisters "tried to pull him together" (30). But his disarray is described from Tabitha's point of view, which her daughters try to force on Tom. Tom is finally whole when he discards the clothes, and forcing him back into them only delays the inevitable. The sister kittens' appeal to the Puddle-Ducks to "Come and button up Tom!" (38) aptly describes the effect of the clothes: to restrain and restrict Tom, and to inhibit his expression of his kitten nature. By this time the sister kittens have lost their clothes, too, and it seems unfair and vengeful of them to insist that Tom wear his clothes while they have shed theirs.

Mr. Drake Puddle-Duck is the first in a line of ingratiating but surly villains whose malevolent potential Potter develops in the course of the

Sawrey books. Though he initially seems to be helping the kittens by retrieving their clothes, he confiscates them and puts on Tom's clothes, and gives the sister kittens' clothes to Jemima and Rebeccah Puddle-Duck. His failure to acknowledge either the kittens' request for help, the fact that he has stolen their clothes, or his ill-looking appearance in Tom's clothes—"They fitted him even worse than Tom Kitten" (42)—underscores the loathsome nature of his manners. He ignores the obvious while asserting civility. His only response to the kittens is "It's a very fine morning!" (42), which belies the fact that he has not been fine, nor will the kittens be, once their mother discovers their misdeeds. The ludicrous sight of him followed by the two other Puddle-Ducks waddling up the road looking preposterously pretentious in the kittens' clothes does nothing to undercut the cool maliciousness that the drake's one line has given him.

When Tabitha finds the kittens "with no clothes on" (46), Potter's line underscores and yet mocks the Victorian horror at nudity. The picture of the three kittens looking naturally kittenlike in their fur comments ironically on Tabitha's silly pretensions of using clothes to make her kittens something they are not. She delivers a peremptory "smack" (49), which may seem harsh in an age that does not always approve of corporal punishment. But Potter was not one to soften actions or their consequences. Furthermore, the spanking is consistent with a cat's discipline of her kittens by cuffing them. Tabitha's explanation of her reaction—"you are not fit to be seen; I am affronted" (49)—contradicts the picture of the kittens looking perfectly presentable and comments ironically on Tabitha's social snobbery. There is nothing offensive about a kitten's private parts or a little disarray in one's fur coat. And there is nothing wrong with a kitten looking or acting like a kitten. Tabitha's prescription for the ideal kitten, one who is seen, perfectly dressed and groomed, but not heard, is as unrealistic for a young cat as it is for a young human. The use of the word "affronted" is another instance of Potter's use of fine language, but it is also particularly accurate for the situation, for it suggests the personal offense Tabitha has taken at the kitten's nudity and the deliberateness that she ascribes to their action.

Potter further comments on the distortions of reality that Tabitha's code of behavior creates, even using authorial intrusion: "I am sorry to say she told her friends that they were in bed with the measles; which was not true" (50). Always one to tell the truth in her books and ever the vigilant observer of the perversions perpetrated by the manners practiced by her parents and their social peers, Potter deplored the telling of such lies and the snobbery they implied. The fact that the mother lies to her guests justifies the havoc the kittens create in the bedroom during their mother's tea party, and the noise they generate in their revenge on their mother's attempts at overproper etiquette. "Somehow there were very extraordinary noises over-head, which disturbed the dignity and repose of the tea party" (53) is Potter's description not of the fun the kittens are having, but of the stultifying boredom that typically characterizes Tabitha's tea parties.

Though one's sympathies tend to run with the kittens, as one might expect in children's literature, yet one senses that the author is not altogether condemning Tabitha for her attempts at propriety. Potter composed *Tom Kitten* just after she bought the farm at Hill Top, and her own pride at proper housekeeping and tasteful decoration is evident in the book. The new clock she had purchased for the main room of the farmhouse is prominently displayed with a proprietor's pride in the picture of Tabitha ushering her kittens upstairs to be washed and dressed. The flowered washbowl which the mother uses and the caned chair on which she stands the kittens to be washed are lovingly and carefully drawn. The profusely flowering garden to which the kittens are exiled is minutely observed in its artistically arranged species-specific blooms. One can feel Potter's approval of Tabitha's wish to provide her guests with an elegant occasion, and her wish to impress them.

But the reader also senses her criticism of such pretentious behavior and of the results of a social code that forces people, especially children, to be what they are not. The cadence of Tabitha's prohibition to the children as they are sent out into the garden strikes the reader as the production of one who heard many such orders peremptorily issued to her in her own childhood. The picture of the kittens' immediate distraction from and disregard for what their mother is saying is the sympathetic response of one whose own youthful reaction was to do as she pleased, in direct contradiction to parental orders. Potter herself wanted to make friends among the villagers at Sawrey; giving proper tea parties would have been one way to ingratiate herself. But, finally, her sympathies lie with the kittens, whose impulse is to have fun. Her dedication of the book "To All Pickles,—Especially to Those That Get Upon My Garden Wall" (7) suggests her pleasure with animal pranks, which overrode almost any other consideration in her life.

Potter's pride in the details of the garden and house is evident from the larger format that she persuaded Warne to use for the book, in order to give adequate attention to individual details about the house and the garden. Her pleasure in the garden, especially in the flowers and shrubs, is obvious, both here and in *The Pie and the Patty-Pan.* In fact, she signals her intention to continue in this house-and-garden mode with her promise near the end of *Tom Kitten* to "tell you more about Tom Kitten" (54), which she did in the following year in *The Roly-Poly Pudding.*

The Tale of the Roly-Poly Pudding

One of Beatrix Potter's great pleasures in owning Hill Top Farm was restoring and refurbishing the house that accompanied the farm buildings and land. In *The Roly-Poly Pudding* she celebrated and preserved that house in her story. The format was larger than usual for her books—five by eight inches, as opposed to four by five inches. She persuaded her publishers to use this larger size in the original edition, showing just how important she considered the story and the illustrations to be. Though the book is now published in the format standard for the Potter collection (in English editions, the story has been retitled *The Tale of Samuel Whiskers*), the larger-sized page originally gave the pictures more prominence and made the minute detail that Potter lavished in the illustrations more evident. The larger format gave the feeling of a book that was more solid, more substantial, though less a part of the Potter canon, which is what the smaller format underscores.

The story concerns the perennial battle of the farm residents against the rats who had invaded and taken up permanent residence in the farmhouse. Tabitha Twitchit, the mother cat of *Tom Kitten* and lady of the house in this story, is conducting her baking, and determines once again to keep her children out of mischief, this time by confining them. But the three—Tom Kitten, Mittens, and Moppet—all escape, Moppet to the flour barrel, Mittens to an empty jar in the dairy, and Tom up the chimney. It is in the chimney that Tom is taken prisoner by Samuel and Anna Maria Whiskers, two insatiable, kleptomaniac rats. They live in the chimney and the attic and steal great quantities of food and odd household items from the human inhabitants of the house, or, in this case, the feline members. Samuel steals some butter and a rolling pin, and Anna Maria steals some dough from Tabitha's baking, carrying it on a saucer that she has "borrowed."[7] The ingredients and utensils are necessary to make Tom Kitten into a rolled pudding, or what is called in the United States a meat pastry. The rats tie Tom up like a rolled roast, smear him with butter, cover him with pastry, and use the rolling pin to smooth out the dough and its stuffing.

By this time Tabitha has noticed that her kittens are missing and has located Moppet and Mittens, who have observed Samuel's and Anna Maria's thefts. Suspecting the worst, she and Cousin Ribby, Mrs. Ribston Pippin of *The Pie and the Patty-Pan* and a visiting neighbor cat, hear a "roly-poly" noise in the attic. When they hear the other kittens' reports of the stolen items, they resolve to call the neighborhood carpenter dog, to remove a floorboard in the attic, where they find Tom before he is baked, but no rats. The Whiskers household has moved to the barn, along with all their things. They continue to flourish there to this day in the form of their many descendants. Moppet and Mittens, being of an entrepreneurial habit of mind, become local rat-catchers, hiring out and charging by the dozens of rats killed, and hanging the tails of their quarry on the barn door to show their prowess. But Tom is permanently intimidated, and spends the rest of his life avoiding rats as much as he can.

The story incorporates many of the characters found in other Potter books, especially those set in Sawrey. Tom Kitten and his sisters are Peter Rabbit and his sisters in feline form. *The Roly-Poly Pudding* is the sequel that Potter had promised her readers in *Tom Kitten*. In a later book the kittens' mother is proprietress of the only other commercial establishment in the village, the one in competition with the shop run by Ginger and Pickles, where credit is not issued. And Ribby is the hostess of a party given in *The Pie and the Patty-Pan*. Gradually, Potter peopled a fantasy transformation of the village of Sawrey with a parallel village full of animals, and thus built a continuity into her series of books. Even Peter Rabbit and Benjamin Bunny eventually remove to the Lake District, first in *Ginger and Pickles*, and later in *Mr. Tod*. However, each of the Sawrey books is complete in its own right, and Potter did not assume that her readers would know of any of the characters beyond the boundaries of a single book. Thus she guaranteed the sales of the individual volume while at the same time assuring continued popularity of her series.

Potter was concerned not only for the popularity and continuation of her books, but also for the perpetuation of her house, both in her books and in the village of Near Sawrey. Her concern for small details in the house at Hill Top is obvious from her will, where she specified not only that the house should remain untouched, but even made arrangements for special items to be placed and displayed in certain rooms in perpetuity. When she refurbished the main living area of the cottage, she wrote to the sister of her publishers, Millie Warne, about specific items that, to this day, remain next to the fireplace at Hill Top: "I have got a pretty dresser with plates on it and some old fashioned chairs; and a warming pan that belonged to my grandmother; and Mrs. Warne's [the publishers' mother] bellows which look well."[8] Though she was concerned with the total effect of the redecoration, individual detail and its contribution to that effect were not beneath her concern: one suspects that she picked out each individual plate on the dresser and arranged them in a specific order to suit her idea of what the room and its decorations should look like. Her involvement with the house was possessive and exacting, and her delight in it endless and yet private. When she married, she and her husband moved to a larger farmhouse on an adjoining farm, partly for the extra space, but also partly for the privacy of the pleasure that Potter found in the cottage at Hill Top. Toward the end of her life she had cleaning help to maintain the cottage, but permitted no one to touch or move anything in the rooms at Hill Top. She kept the building specifically for her own use and wanted no one to disturb her things or her privacy while she was there.

In 1906 and 1907, when she was composing and drawing the story of *The Roly-Poly Pudding,* she had only just purchased the farm and the house and was making extensive renovations to the property. One of the fascinating aspects of the house was its large, thick walls, of seventeenth-century origin and of massive depth. Over the years before Potter purchased it, the farm needed more maintenance than it received, and she sought to rectify the neglect while also keeping the character of the house. Part of this character, unfortunately, was a great population of rats, who had had free run of the house and had developed many secret tunnels and hiding places which, penetrating as they did through the main structure were hard to find and eliminate.

Initially, Potter was sympathetic to the rats, whom she had known as a race since her lonely childhood in the third-floor nursery. Mrs. Cannon, the wife of the farm's manager, proposed the acquisition of a number of cats, the idea of which horrified Potter. But as the extent of the nuisance became obvious to her, she gradually acquiesced. In the story Samuel and Anna Maria "borrow" a saucer, but one suspects that the loan is permanent. When they move out of the house to the barn, they take with them "our property—and other people's"(60). Once again they "borrow" from Miss Potter, who is here a clear presence in the story, this time taking a wheelbarrow to move their things. The author's shock at their acquisition and her uncustomary intrusion into the story, both in narrative and illustration, indicates not only her humorous response to the rats' appropriations of her property, but also her amazement that they should acquire so many large items from the farm: "I am sure *I* never gave her leave to borrow my wheel-barrow!" (66). That the rats should have in their baggage half a smoked ham from the kitchen, and that they should be fiercesome enough to imprison a kitten, especially one as mischievous as Tom, shows just how menacing, while at the same time amusing, their occupation of the house was. But that Potter gives them long, prosperous lives, to the detriment of Farmer Potatoes's fodder in the barn, indicates that, as long as they stayed outside the house, Potter had no quarrel with their ratlike behavior and only wished them well:

> They eat up the chicken food, and steal the oats and bran, and make holes in the meal bags.
> And they are all descended from Mr. and Mrs. Samuel Whiskers—children and grand-children and great grand-children!
> There is no end to them!
>
> (71)

On the other hand, she does pose an end to them, in the business by which Moppet and Mittens make their living: rat-catching. It is simply in the nature of nature and conduct of farming that cats and humans will be the enemies of rats. But Potter does spare her own and the reader's feelings by not showing the extermination of Samuel and Maria Whiskers, and by describing the success of their posterity. Moppet's and Mittens's victims are no particular rats and are, indeed reduced simply to their tails, to show both the reader and prospective employers how well the cats do their jobs.

This extension of the ending beyond the actual demands of the plots was becoming characteristic of Potter's books, as if she were daring the limits of her readers and publishers. The reward of the rabbit sisters and the punishment of Peter by doses of camomile tea began this tendency. *Tom Kitten* goes on long enough to show the banishment of the kittens to the bedroom, supposedly overcome by measles, and long enough to explain what the ducks do to their clothes. This time Potter gives each of the kittens, and the rats as well, lives to live beyond the

rescue of Tom and the "happily ever after." The sister kittens have
professions, and the rats are nearly promised life eternal, at least by
their ability to live on in their progeny. As with the development of
more and more threatening villains, Potter is also showing greater self-
assurance in the creation of her stories. Her editors could no longer do
anything more than suggest alternatives, so sure was her sense of plot
and character.

The Roly-Poly Pudding seems to some readers ominous, with its foreshadowing of the difficulties Tom will encounter up the chimney sig-
naling a growing tension over Tom's fate: "Now this is what had been
happening to Tom Kitten, and it shows how very unwise it is to go up
a chimney in a very old house, where a person does not know his way,
and where there are enormous rats" (29). Margaret Lane claims that it
is the best of Potter's "great near-tragedies,"[9] a term originated by
Grahame Greene.[10] Lane notes Potter's willingness to frighten her readers. It is true that there are a number of possibly fatal ends confronting
Tom: incineration in the chimney if the newly started fire catches him,
abandonment under the attic floorboards, where he is so tightly tied
up that he can neither move nor call out for help, or cooking to death
as the main course of the rats' dinner. The mutton bones that he finds
in the chimney, where the rats are storing them, foreshadow Tom's own
skeletal remains after his death. But the entire situation is so preposterous that Tom's dismal end seems unlikely. Samuel and Anna Maria
are pictured as rats of substance, with plenty of girth and enough power to roll a rolling pin up the stairs to the attic. Yet it seems outrageous
that they could actually frighten even a young kitten and tie him up.
Samuel's portliness make him an object of the reader's laughter. And
his arguments with Anna Maria over the proper way to prepare a pudding hardly make him sinister. Though the story could be ghastly, yet
from the beginning Potter creates an outlandish scene where, though
the reader is clearly in the realm of fantasy, even so, common sense
intervenes to mitigate any genuine threat.

The story contains one of the few occasions when Potter actually put
herself in the story. But Tabitha Twitchit is not Beatrix Potter, and
perhaps the author's own fiercely proprietary interest in the house com-
pelled her to assert her own presence in the story. Though the story is
clearly about animals, yet two of the characters are modeled after Sawrey residents: John Joiner, the efficient carpenter dog, was John Taylor,
a local fix-it man from whom, in all likelihood, Potter did order a
wheelbarrow and two hen-coops, as the story says. And the photograph

of the original for Farmer Potatoes is still in existence and allows identification of the model as John Postlethwaite, a neighbor. Potter wisely
used a photographic model, rather than simply sketching, as she did
with Mr. McGregor, for the result is a convincing portrait of a real
farmer, rather than a caricature. With equal wisdom, she placed her
self-portrait in the far distance, with the figures of Samuel and Anna
Maria in the foreground. They are pushing the "borrowed" wheelbarrow and they clearly upstage Potter and do not allow the illustrator's
intrusion into her own illustration to dominate either the picture or
the end of the story. In fact, she is so unclearly portrayed that it is
difficult to see whether the figure is really a human, much less a portrait of Potter. The identification comes in the text: "And when I was
going to the post late in the afternoon—I looked up the lane from the
corner, and I saw Mr. Samuel Whiskers and his wife . . ." (66). The
wheelbarrow may be hers, but the picture, and indeed the rest of the
story, belong to the rats.

The plenitude of pictures, both in color and in black and white,
indicates Potter's willingness to spend time drawing and redrawing the
interior of the house she loved so well. And her ability to draw the
house from a cat's perspective shows her careful consideration of the
house from all different angles, not just her own. Her drawing of Anna
Maria's scurry along the floor in front of the dresser with the pretty
plates indicates that if she did not get down on the floor herself to do
the drawing, she was able to contemplate and observe what the room
and the dresser would look like from the rat's perspective. Her drawings make the house look grand and spacious, in contrast to the small,
cozy sense it has for humans. But from the point of view of cats, the
house truly is large. And her two drawings that include the bannister
and spindles on the stairway to the second floor imply her admiration
for the carpentry and her affection for the claret-colored curtains which
she hung in the window on the landing. Finally, her picture of the
view of the countryside from the top of the chimney suggests that, in
her rummaging about the house, and in the process of repair, she actually climbed on the roof herself to see what Tom Kitten sees. Her
appreciation of the house not only extended to its small details, but
also to its perspective from different points of view, literally, from the
floor to the roof.

Her willingness to design special endpapers, included in the first
editions, but not in present ones, indicates the care with which she
designed the whole book. This is not just another book in the Peter

Rabbit series, but rather a special one, deserving not only special end-papers, but also a special design for the title page. On the back of the half-title page of the original edition is a coat of arms for the Whiskers family, forming the top of a bookplate, with the family motto *"Resurgam!!!"* [I will rise again].[11] The dedication page, included in modern editions, shows a picture of "Sammy," the pet mouse who was the model for Samuel Whiskers. The original title page includes above the title the color picture of Samuel sitting on a rolling pin, in modern editions in black and white. Scrollwork encompasses Moppet, Mittens, and Tom in his pastry crust observed by mice on either side, all placed below the title. Beneath her byline Potter included an ironic pictorial comment. Though she gives herself the credit of being "Author of 'The Tale of Peter Rabbit'" (5), her other works are encompassed by a terse "etc." followed by a line of four identical bunny figures, as if to indicate her fatigue with those "wearisome rabbits."[12]

The book celebrates Potter's love, not only of the house, but of the way of life it represented for her, full of antiquity and order in her own house, with all of her special things exactly where she wanted them. For a woman who grew up in a house dominated solely by her parents and their wishes about arrangements, the owning of such a house must have been a great accomplishment. That the house should have included a population of rodents was a mere difficulty, and hardly an insurmountable one. Potter cherished the interruptions and impositions of that "Persecuted (But Irrepressible) Race," as she called the rats in her dedication (2) so long as they did no real harm.

The Tale of Jemima Puddle-Duck

Jemima Puddle-Duck is Beatrix Potter's "poem about the farm," as Margaret Lane describes it.[13] It is the first of her books set wholly and unequivocally at Hill Top Farm among the farm animals. It features as part of its panoramic background buildings and vistas specific to the farm and to the country around Near Sawrey. Those who visit Near Sawrey today will find little changed in the more than seventy years that have passed since the book was written. The stasis is due not only to Potter's heroic efforts to preserve the farm and the way of life she enjoyed in Near Sawrey during her own time. It also results from the simple lack of change and inevitability of that way of life in that particular part of the country. Though the land might have become more commercialized for tourists, the visitors come mostly during the summer months. During the rest of the year farm life, unmodernized by agribusiness, proceeds, and the lifestyle remains unchanged.

In the story Jemima leaves the farm in desperation to find a safe nesting place in which to hatch her eggs. She finds what she considers the perfect location, in the woods, but meets a gentleman with elegant manners and "sandy coloured whiskers,"[14] who talks the naive duck into laying her brood in his home. After she lays them over the course of a number of days, he invites her to a party before she officially begins to sit on them. As she is gathering provisions for the party, she meets the farm collie, Kep. He is suspicious of Jemima's absences and of the nature of her provisions, which seem to him all that is necessary to stuff a duck for roasting. He calls two foxhounds to his aid. Together the three dogs find the fox's home, rout the fox, who is never heard of again, and destroy Jemima's eggs by eating them themselves. In recompense Jemima is allowed to hatch her next set of eggs herself, but the result is an unsatisfactory four out of the whole brood of eggs, owing, as Jemima says, to her nervousness.

Like Mrs. Rabbit in *Peter Rabbit,* Jemima Puddle-Duck is a character set in some not-too-distant but still remote past. Her shawl may have been typical dress for a farm lady of Potter's period, but the poke bonnet dates her as a resident of the past. The fox, never named as such, but always described as the gentleman "with the sandy coloured whiskers" (22), wears a coat with a long tail. He cultivates manners so exquisitely proper that he, too, places himself in that uncertain past. As Potter pointed out, the story is a revision of the fairy tale "Little Red-Riding Hood" and thus properly belongs in a period "once upon a time," in any time but now.

Jemima is also modeled after a particularly quirky duck who lived on Potter's farm. She was known for trying to evade the farmer's wife and her children in their attempts to locate her eggs and take them away from her before she had a chance to mismanage their incubation. Mrs. Cannon, the wife of the tenant manager who ran Hill Top Farm in Potter's absence, was in the habit of confiscating the ducks' eggs and letting hens incubate them, ducks being, in her estimation, poor sitters and likely to abandon their eggs.

Though Jemima is rescued at the end, and there is something of a happy ending in the four new ducklings, still the story is one of Potter's more ominous. Jemima is such an innocent, so headstrong, that the reader doubts her judgment from the beginning. When she meets the gentleman, her inability to see through his invitation to sit on her eggs at his home further places her well-being in jeopardy and increases tension about the outcome. That the fox's home is placed among the foxgloves is a sure sign to the reader that the gentleman is really no gentleman, but a fox. The gentleman is described as sitting on his tail, owing to the dampness, another ominous indicator of his real identity.

When the reader encounters the first picture of the fox in full view, no longer hiding behind his newspaper, his tail is obvious to the viewer, if not to Jemima. But in the next picture she is following him up the path to his house, and his tail is in her full view. Her inability to divine his true identity in spite of the evidence at that point becomes truly threatening. The added detail that he has a "sackful of feathers" (29) only further manifests Jemima's peril. Jemima wonders at the presence of the feathers, but comes to no conclusion herself. The fact that she nearly smothers in the quantity of feathers in the woodshed suggests her demise if she does not avert the threat to herself and her eggs, but Jemima again does not draw any conclusions. The gentleman's invitation to join him for a party where the repast will be an omelette leads the reader to ask whence the eggs will come and suggests the likely possibility that the fox will be using Jemima's eggs, in spite of his avowed fondness for ducklings, which Jemima takes at face value. That he orders her to collect herbs that are typically used for stuffing a duck is the crowning irony and ultimate horror, couched in rude manners which again Jemima notes but does not probe.

At the point where she begins to gather the herbs Potter shows her without the bonnet and shawl that make her a proper lady-duck. Without the clothes she becomes simply a domesticated duck, nothing standing between her and dinner except slaughter and plucking. In the final picture of the mother duck with her four ducklings, again she does not have her shawl and bonnet, reverting to her true nature as a mother duck. But Jemima without her clothes is not as interesting as she is when she is human. There is no story left to tell about her once she becomes simply a duck. She is much more interesting as a naive if eccentric lady.

Though there is the moderately happy ending to the story, still Jemima has lost the first brood of eggs, and the second brood has not been as successful as might have been expected. The rescue of Jemima by the dogs recalls the rescue of Little Red Riding-Hood by the woodsman in the Grimm brothers' version of the story. But the sacrifice of many unborn ducklings implies that Potter's model is more likely Perrault's earlier and more grisly version. In that version Red Riding-Hood is eaten as a punishment for her misbehavior of talking to a wolf in the forest and for her further transgression of curiosity about his prominent features. At the end, Jemima is chastised, returned with a guard of dog escorts to the farmyard, in public humiliation. Though she is saved, she still must sacrifice her silly idea of finding a nest away from the farm. The rescue is not the happy ending one finds at the end of the Grimms' version of "Red Riding-Hood."

The loss of the ducklings is sad for the duck as well as the reader, especially the child reader whose sympathies might naturally be expected to lie with the helpless egg-ducklings. It is likely, as Margaret Lane pointed out, that Potter felt obliged to end the story happily, for the sake of Ralph and Betsy Cannon, the children of her farm's manager and the people to whom the story was dedicated.[15] Though she did not avoid horrific implications and grisly details it must have seemed unthinkable to let Jemima end as a bloody mess in the fox's lair, especially with children watching. Jemima is punished, but the harshness of the justice is mitigated to some degree by the fact that she is allowed one more chance to hatch a brood herself.

In the pictures one sees many of the details of farm life at Hill Top. As if to do justice to the barn as she had to the house in her earlier books, Potter even shows the reader its interior, with livestock and fowl in their usual places. Mrs. Cannon, in the story described as the tyrannical farmer's wife who will not let the ducks hatch their own eggs, is seen in the doorway leading to the back yard. Ralph and Betsy Cannon, her children, stand at the wrought-iron gate to the kitchen garden and retrieve Jemima's eggs from their hiding places in the rhubarb so that the hens can take over the job of hatching them. This is one instance in Potter's stories where humans deliberately intrude themselves into the lives of the animals. In *Peter Rabbit* and its sequels the rabbits intrude themselves upon the humans. But, as Potter knew, she was not particularly adept at drawing human characters. Mrs. Cannon is awkwardly posed about the arms, as is the boy, Ralph. Their heads do not seem to fit well on their shoulders. So, after the two pictures showing the Cannon family, which occur at the beginning of the book, humans do not reappear, except in the background behind the cart in front of the Tower Bank Arms (44).

In that picture the foxhounds in front of the cart and the sign over the doorway to the inn are the focal points. The man unloading the cart is simply part of the scenery, and the story will soon depart from human environs to pursue the sandy-whiskered gentleman. In fact, to keep the humans at the farm from becoming too prominent in the story, Potter immediately moves the scene to an unspecified location but, to Jemima, a secret place in the woods around the farm, away from the intervention of humans. Thus the Cannon children cannot confiscate Jemima's eggs, but Jemima is still close enough so that the dogs can find and rescue her.

The story shows Potter at her finest in portraying the details of life at Hill Top and her love for the picturesque details of the village of Near Sawrey. But because of the archetypical model of the story—the helpless and naive beguiled but rescued from seeming self-destruction by the loyal and dependable—Potter manages to make this more than just a story of local color and interest. It is, as the dedication says, a "Farmyard Tale" (7) with implications about self-preservation and shrewdness as admirable virtues. Grahame Greene suggests that at this point in her life she suffered some kind of mental breakdown, given the ominous gloom he finds in the character of the sandy-whiskered gentleman.[16] More likely she was simply coming to terms with life on the farm, where wild animals invade the domain of the domesticated ones and where death, if not always so threatening, was still part of the business of running a farm.

Ginger and Pickles

If *Jemima Puddle-Duck* is Beatrix Potter's story about farmlife in Sawrey and *The Roly-Poly Pudding* is her celebration of her farmhouse, then *Ginger and Pickles* is her celebration of village life, especially as it revolves around the main center of attraction and social life, the village store. The title of the book is not only the name of the establishment in Potter's fictionalized version of Near Sawrey, it is also the name of the two proprietors, a tomcat and a terrier, respectively. In this book Potter not only preserves in her fiction many of the people she has come to know in the village, she also portrays a new preoccupation that she found dominating her life since she had become a landowner and businesswoman: how to make a profit, and how to keep accounts. The book brings back many familiar characters from earlier Potter books as patrons of the store, at the same time that it introduces this new concern for bookkeeping and solvency while dealing with one's neighbors as clients.

As the proprietors of the village store, Ginger and Pickles are notorious in the village for their lax credit policies. In fact, though their sales are prodigious, they have no money since everyone buys on credit and no one ever pays. The lack of cash brings the two shopkeepers to eating their own stock in order to stay alive. When the first of the year arrives, and Pickles must renew his dog license and the taxes must be paid, the two find themselves in a real "pickle." For the government does not run its business along such credit policies, and Pickles is unable to get a new license on credit. The two shopkeepers think themselves harassed by the local policeman-doll, who comes to leave the tax bill and whom they suspect of going to get a real policeman. They shut down the business and go their separate ways, but the shop is reopened by Sally Henny Penny, who cannot make change without becoming flustered, and by a number of other local entrepreneurs, who sell candles and peppermints, but who are not exactly models of business integrity in the quality of their products. Elsewhere in her writing, especially her correspondence, Potter used the word "pickle" to describe a scamp or a well-intentioned creator of havoc. She used the word especially to apply to animals whose physical exploits led them to embarrassing situations. The name as used here implies for the reader knowledgeable in the corpus of Potter's works, that neither Ginger, nor Pickles, nor their enterprise will turn out well. And indeed their method of doing business is hardly businesslike and leads to the eventual dissolution of their partnership.

The root of the problem for the "Ginger and Pickles" establishment is the idea of credit, which Potter duly explains to her child readers:

> Now the meaning of "credit" is this—when a customer buys a bar of soap, instead of pulling out a purse and paying for it—she says she will pay another time.
> And Pickles makes a low bow and says, "With pleasure, madam," and it is written down in a book.
> The customers come again and again, and buy quantities, in spite of being afraid of Ginger and Pickles.[17]

The description shows the meaning of credit for Ginger and Pickles and shows a child exactly why credit is so attractive: because Potter makes no mention of repayment, and the animals in the story have no intention of paying. Thus, when Potter describes business at this store in this way—"The customers came in crowds every day and bought quantities" (22)—the irony, at least for the adult reader, is clear: there are no real sales to customers, just imprudent gifts made by the proprietors. So when Potter describes the "sales" as "Enormous, ten times as large as Tabitha Twitchit's" (25), the only other shopkeeper in the village and one who insists on cash sales, the reader understands that the large sales do not indicate financial well-being for the establishment of Ginger and Pickles.

The pictures underscore the pilfering that is going on in the name of business. The shop is filled with familiar characters. The story opens with Lucinda and Jane, the dolls from *Two Bad Mice*, as the first customers. The policeman-doll who delivers the rates and taxes is also taken from that earlier story. One sees inside the store Peter Rabbit and Benjamin and two of Peter's sisters, identifiable by their red cloaks. Jeremy Fisher is trying on new galoshes and Mrs. Tiggy-Winkle is the customer who comes in to buy a bar of soap on credit. Ptolemy Tortoise follows Peter into the store in another picture, and outside, Jemima Puddle-Duck gossips with Sally Henny Penny, who are surrounded by their broods of yellow chicks and ducklings. Squirrel Nutkin and a friend appear to be stealing nuts, as they were wont to do in their story. The rats, whether Samuel and Anna Maria Whiskers or other unclothed, unidentified thieves, are everywhere, especially in the endpapers, which are different from Potter's usual inclusion of a frame of characters from earlier books surrounding the white space appropriate for a bookplate. In these endpapers the rats, or perhaps they are mice, are helping a friend who is stuck in a bottle to extricate himself, wantonly making free use of the shop's twine to fashion a lifeline. On the back papers Ptolemy Tortoise and Jeremy Fisher are playing with the balance used for determining weights and measures, as are the mice on the facing page. The rodents seem as likely to abscond with the coins used for weights as they are with the biscuits and wafers they contemplate in one of the pictures in the book. One has the feeling that the smaller animals have free access to the store, and their movements are not controlled either during shop hours or after hours. Thus, when Ginger says that the mice tempt him, he may be showing good customer relations by asking Pickles to wait on them, so that the cat will not offend anyone or lose business by eating the customers. On the other hand, the suspension of his good cat sense in favor of his somewhat feeble business acumen is doing the enterprise as much harm as his eating of the mice would. As Pickles notes, if Ginger ate the mice, they would not go to the competitor's shop. In fact, they would not go anywhere (14), which might be a blessing for the store's stocks.

The colored drawings for the book are much more vivid and varied in their tones than in other Potter stories, but perhaps this is because the animals here are not pursuing animal lives, with the exception of the mice, who are generally not shown wearing clothing as they follow their natural inclinations to raid the stores. Instead, these animals are behaving distinctly as humans, except when Ginger and Pickles admit their natural taste for some of the rabbit and mice customers. Shopping and shopkeeping are human pursuits, and so these animals are shown wearing human clothes. The colors of these clothes are all artificial, with no attempt to make the animals fit into nature by giving them clothing of natural browns and greens. Peter Rabbit's blue coat is definitely a man-made blue. Instead of wearing the more neutral black clogs of his own book, on the cover to *Ginger and Pickles* he wears red pumps. The walls of the shop are painted a brilliant green in contrast to the more muted, subtle tones that Potter used in other books in the woodland scenes. And the brick walls of the shop are fuchsia in color, as are the shawls of Jemima Puddle-Duck and Mrs. Tiggy-Winkle, and the tablecloths and chair in Ginger and Pickles' business office. Though fuchsia does occur in nature, it is not usual except in hybrid plants and a few wildflowers. Its prominence in this book points to Potter's design to record human village life through her animals, rather than to place her animals in a fantasy world that is parallel to the human realm. That the toy policeman-doll might summon a real policeman, and that Ginger and Pickles cast their accounts in pounds sterling indicates that this book describes human beings more than it does animals.

The book ends in one of Potter's most extended codas to any book. The story goes fully twenty pages beyond the closing of the shop by the cat and dog. Both animals find careers afterwards, and the shop changes hands. Their customers go on to several different provisioners, and suffer from these businesspersons' foibles, such as Sally Henny Penny's "Grand co-operative Jumble" (70–73) and the unwillingness of the mice to follow the customary practice of taking back the unburnt ends of candles when their customers were finished with them. The dependence of any town on its shopkeepers, especially a small village where contact with the outside world was limited, is focal, for both patrons and proprietors. And for a small village the peculiarities of the shopkeepers would have been a subject of great interest and gossip. The lengthiness of the ending has much of the ungainly shapelessness of human gossip; it rambles on, and yet fittingly so, given the humanness of the story and its interest. Shopkeeping and all the accoutrements of a general store had long been thought appropriate materials for children, as seen in the many German toy books, with pop-up, fold-out pages full of the many products that such a general store would have. Yet here Potter gives her child readers a glimpse of what adults would also have found interesting about a store: the social life that revolves around it and the quirks of the residents of the village.

The Tale of Mrs. Tittlemouse

At the end of *The Flopsy Bunnies* Potter had invented a resourceful heroine who, like the mouse in Aesop's fable about the lion and the mouse, rescued from capture another creature by gnawing away at the fibers that the humans had used to imprison him. Mrs. Tittlemouse is not a focal character in *The Flopsy Bunnies,* but the last picture in the book is of her, completely clothed in garments made of the rabbit wool donated by the Flopsy Bunnies in gratitude for her heroism. Here was a character already created, if not yet adequately personified, just waiting for her story to be told, and in the year following the publication of *The Flopsy Bunnies* Potter decided to tell her story.

Personification of mice and inventing stories about them had always come easily and felicitously to Potter, and *Mrs. Tittlemouse* was no exception. A wood mouse, as opposed to the house-mouse, urban nature of the mice of Gloucester or of the dollhouse in *Two Bad Mice,* Mrs. Tittlemouse lives in a neat mouse hole in the woods near Sawrey. She is particularly fastidious in her housekeeping, like Mrs. Rabbit. But Mrs. Tittlemouse lives alone, without the complication of family members to create havoc with her orderliness. Unfortunately, she has a variety of unwanted guests, primarily of the insect variety, who let themselves in without her leave and are eradicated only by Mr. Jackson, the neighborhood toad. He also comes to call unannounced and, though he eliminates insects, he also tracks up the floor with his muddy feet. He is not gracious enough to eat whatever Mrs. Tittlemouse serves him, but demands, however politely, honey for his meal. When both the insects and the toad are finally gone, Mrs. Tittlemouse exorcises their lingering presences by a thorough housecleaning and then a party for her friends. She also takes precautions against toad invasions in the future by narrowing the hole that serves as entrance to her home so that the frog no longer has access.

The evident approval with which Potter describes the domestic arrangements of the wood mouse would seem to have its source in her own pleasure in owning and ordering a place of her own at Hill Top Farm. The mouse home is much like the cottage at the farm, with low ceilings and small rooms and well-stocked kitchen stores. The details with which Potter enumerates the many virtues of such an unpretentious home stem from her own growing affection for housekeeping, or at least for its end result. One suspects that Mrs. Tittlemouse's horror in finding infestations of bumblebees, ladybugs, spiders, butterflies, and lice derives from the author's abhorrence of such intrusions upon the order she worked so hard to create in the old farmhouse. But the precision with which she drew the insect intruders is not the careful observation that a housekeeper typically gives such intruders. Rather, Potter's source for her drawings was the many wildlife and entymological studies she did in her early adulthood both in natural settings and in the Victoria and Albert Museum. While casting about for a worthy life's pursuit, she was also storing up an appreciation for the precise illustration even of the obnoxious, and she spares no detail of antennae or groping limb when she draws her bugs. Fortunately, the bugs here are not supposed to be sympathetic characters, but rather insubordinate, rude, uninvited guests. It is difficult for any artist to draw a bug both precisely and sympathetically, and the crawling, unpleasant detail with which Potter rendered her insects only underscores the unpleasantness of their visits and the peace that prevails once they are banished.

Mrs. Tittlemouse's cathartic, almost ritual cleansing of the house after her visitors' departure seems to resonate with Potter's own pleasure in doing such housecleaning herself. Her life at her parents' home was dominated by dependence on a household staff who both enervated the inhabitants by leaving them with nothing to do and by disempowering them in their own home. The servants both tyrannized and enraged the Potters by being unreliable or unwilling to do the housework in the exact fashion that Mrs. Potter wanted. In her own labor in cleaning and refurbishing the cottage at Hill Top Potter found a new activity that had benefits in providing useful activity and in enabling one to control one's own environment. There were also emotional benefits in the job when finished, for the result was the preservation and refurbishing of antique objects and an old building that might otherwise have been lost. Potter herself enjoyed the cathartic effect of scrubbing and polishing, and a new pleasure in keeping these newly cleaned objects in the precise order she wanted. Her ability to exclude unwanted visitors to Hill Top, whether animal, insect, or human, was as

much cherished by the author as by the wood mouse. Mrs. Tittlemouse's assertion of power over her own domain by simple housewifely
measures must surely have resonated in Potter's own sense of herself as
sole inhabitant of Hill Top.

But the fact is that neither Mrs. Tittlemouse nor Potter could ex-
terminate the unwanted guests; all that either of them could do was to
take precautions against further invasion of the housekeepers' domains.
For all that the insects were abhorrent, yet they were still beautiful,
still worthy of preserving, either in picture or in nature.

Potter and her editor at the Warne publishing house were divided
over the inclusion of lice, "creepy crawly people," as Potter called them
in the manuscript version of the story,[18] though the point seems trivial
from the modern reader's vantage point. The invading spider is gro-
tesque enough that almost anything else would seem not nearly so
disgusting by comparison. Yet Potter acquiesced and eliminated them
in the final draft. She also changed an earwig to a beetle. The point of
all these insects is that they are offensive, especially so for girls, to
whom Potter thought the book would most likely appeal. The editor's
reasons for objecting are not clear, but his attempts to avoid offending
the reader are misplaced: there was nothing that Potter wanted more
of this book than a truly offended, horrified reaction to the invasion of
the insects.

The Tale of Pigling Bland

As the last of the Sawrey books to be written during her period of
phenomenal production, Beatrix Potter chose to write a love story. In
keeping with the increasing complexity of her plots and the growing
malignity of her villains, in *Pigling Bland* it is not natural, innate
animosity of one species of animal for another that causes the conflict.
Instead, it is man's use—and abuse—of farm livestock that sets the
story's villainy in motion. Though the hero and heroine, both pigs,
find happiness at the end, it is by evading the humans who threaten
to make them into bacon that their happiness is finally realized.
Though Potter herself denied that the happy couple is modeled after
herself and her husband-to-be, she did admit that they took long walks
along the same path that Pigling Bland and his girl-pig used. The
comic ending of the dance and imminent marriage suggest that a similar escape into happily-ever-after was in store for her with marriage to
William Heelis.

The love story does not begin as one; on Miss Potter's farm there is a family of pigs, so large and so mischievous that some of the piglings must be sold in order that the remaining members may eat. From the litter, two males are singled out to go to market: Pigling Bland and his brother Alexander. Each is spruced up and dressed in clothes for market, and sent on his way with a license and a list of aphorisms to guide him. Though the two make some progress on the road, Alexander misplaces his license and is sent back to the farm. Pigling Bland continues on his own until he is wet and tired, and crawls into a chicken coop for nighttime shelter.

Unfortunately for Pigling, the coop belongs to Peter Thomas Piperson, of the nursery rhyme "Tom, Tom, the Piper's son," who "stole a pig and away he run." Tom takes Pigling into custody in his farmhouse, where Pigling finds another stolen piglet, this one a young lady. Both determine to run away to the county border, which they succeed in doing in spite of the last-minute attempts of a grocer to return them to their owners and collect a reward for them. The closing scene shows them dancing together; presumably now that both are "over the hills and far away,"[19] Pigling will realize his dream of farming potatoes.

The story poses a clear contrast between Potter's feelings for her animals as a farmer and her feelings for her characters. Hill Top was becoming known for its excellent pigs. But the purpose of raising pigs is to send them to slaughter. At one point, Potter deliberately violated the preferences of her farm's manager and breeder of pigs and bought an unpedigreed female piglet, which she kept as a pet. Though she took pride in her farm's growing reputation, she also recognized many of the farm animals as individuals. None of them faded into the herd under her careful, remembering gaze. But still, she could be objective about her livestock, and could change her attitude, especially when money was involved. As she wrote to Millie Warne about an early farming triumph with her stock, "The two biggest little pigs have been sold, which takes away from the completeness of the family group. But they have fetched a good price, and their appetites were fearful—five meals a day and not satisfied."[20]

It is this curious ambivalence about her pigs' future that one sees in the book, both in the attitude of the piglets' mother, Aunt Pettitoes, and in the attitude of Miss Potter herself, who appears in the book. Potter as a character in the book finds the pigs a particular nuisance, in their mischief and invasion of the garden and the laundry. Her own voice reproves Aunt Pettitoes: "Aunt Pettitoes, Aunt Pettitoes you are a worthy person, but your family is not well brought up. Every one of them has been in mischief except Spot and Pigling Bland." Aunt Pettitoes does not defend the behavior of her brood or refute the claims of her owner. Instead, she gives yet another reason to dispose of them: "Four little boy pigs and four little girl pigs are too many altogether . . . there will be more to eat without them" (15). Though the reader might have expected possessive motherliness from Aunt Pettitoes, one finds a businesslike attitude and a certain self-interest in the sow. She keeps one of the brood at home to do the housework, and her motivation for sending her children off shows no evidence of self-sacrifice. She wants more to eat herself and will sacrifice her children for that end if necessary. Potter as a character tries to help Aunt Pettitoes with her unruly clan, by chasing them out of the garden, helping with them on laundry day, and rescuing Alexander from the pig trough. But the two ladies are allied in their practical outlook toward the piglets, one which in some ways smacks of the heartless practicality of Hansel and Gretel's mother in abandoning her children.

Aunt Pettitoes does not let Alexander and Pigling go to market without feeling; in fact, she weeps over them and, like Shakespeare's Polonius, hands over to them her collective wisdom about pig life before they leave: "Mind your Sunday clothes, and remember to blow your nose . . . beware of traps, hen roosts, bacon and eggs; always walk upon your hind legs. . . . Observe sign-posts and milestones; do not gobble herring bones" (17–18, 21), a list that is likely to continue, except for Potter's interruption. The internal rhymes in her advice— clothes and nose, eggs and legs, milestones and bones—give the regulations an automatic quality of unexamined truisms, but the prohibitions give structure to the rest of Pigling's story. It is in the chicken coop that he meets Tom Piperson's trap. The hens in the coop remark about the irony of his presence in their domain by cackling, "bacon and eggs" (41). And it is because both he and the girl-pig he will meet have clothes that their story is told at all, for they are exceptionally attractive pigs when they are dressed as humans and not dressed the way a pig's carcass is dressed. That they are upright on their hind legs gives them the literal perspective to see "over the hills and far away" (94) as well as the means to run away and dance in the final scene. Though the pigs find little temptation to eat fish, yet their observation of the road markers indicates to them how far away they are from home and how to get to their ultimate destinations, either the market or the county border.

Potter's advice sounds the ominous note of banishment, of exclusion from childhood, of Adam and Eve's eviction from the Garden of Eden: "if you once cross the county boundary you cannot come back" (21). The prohibition sounds like a local regulation having to do with local livestock competition and disease control, especially when it is coupled with the licenses that the pigs must carry with them. But still, it seems particularly severe, especially for such young and tearful pigs. Though Pigling is banished from childhood from the county boundary onward, yet it is that boundary that promises him freedom. He and Pig-Wig have no desire to return, for their fate lies in happily ever after, over the hills and far away.

Pigling Bland and not Alexander is the hero of the story. These two piglets are singled out from the rest of the brood at the opening of the story because they are the only two of the litter who have humanlike names. The others have alliterative labels—Suck-suck, Yock-Yock, Chin-chin—or descriptions of their appearance or personality—Spot, Stumpy, and Cross-patch. Alexander as a name suggests high calling and important destiny, but he is excluded from heroism from the beginning because of his folly in being trapped in the pig trough. He is later described as "hopelessly volatile" (23) because he does not listen to the good advice before he leaves home and because of his incessant giggling at a very serious moment in his life. He gobbles up the food provided for the entire trip within the first mile of home, in contrast to Pigling Bland, who protests that he will not share his own provisions because "I wish to preserve them for emergencies" (28). Thus, it is not surprising that Alexander loses track of his license and is taken home by the policeman in disgrace. Pigling is left to pursue the road to market by himself, and the departure of his brother leaves him free to act out his destiny without interference.

The many nursery rhymes that inspire and are recalled in this story suggest that Pigling's market destination is an ambiguous one. Potter implies that he is going to a "hiring fair" (34), where he will find future employment. And the nursery rhyme that the story calls to mind, "This little pig went to market," does not imply any intention to see the pig slaughtered. But the other rhymes that the story suggests imply more dreadful ends. "Tom, Tom, the Piper's son" steals a pig and runs away with it. In another rhyme the unseen narrator goes "To market, to market, to buy a fat pig" and returns "Home again, home again, jigetty jig."[21] To the farmer, sending a pig to market means putting it up for sale, either for breeding stock or for slaughter. When

Potter says of Alexander that she "disposed of Alexander in the neighborhood; he did fairly well when he had settled down" (33), it is not clear whether he did well as a breeder, or whether he did well as a candidate for slaughtering. Pigling Bland does not wish to undergo the indignity of "standing all by himself in a crowded market, to be stared at, pushed, and hired by some big strange farmer" (34–35). But farmers are invasive of personal dignity whether they are hiring help or purchasing livestock. It is not clear whether the little pig is naive about his fate, or whether Potter is trying to mitigate his end by providing a fantasy solution in a farmhand's job.

Pigling's wish to "have a little garden and grow potatoes" (35) is appropriate for him in his pig's predilection for potatoes and in the idea of the garden as paradise. The small size of the desire well fits a piglet whose last name suggests his mild-mannered lack of pretension. It also suggests Potter's own desire for a small retreat into anonymity. Gardens, both vegetable and flower, had been a prominent part of her books as well as her farm. Her wish to retreat to one mirrors her desire to escape from the strictures of her parents to become a farmer, to a place where no one would suspect that she was the famous Miss Potter.

In Peter Thomas Piperson the reader finds not only the villain of the story but also the hero's release. Named for two nursery-rhyme characters simultaneously, Peter Piper, whose rhyme has no bearing here but to suggest an alliterative, compound name, and Tom, the Piper's son, this villain is one of Potter's most sinister because he is human. Unlike Mr. McGregor, he is rude, telling Pig-Wig to "Shut up!" while she is locked in the closet (46), and rummaging intrusively through Pigling Bland's pockets while he is still wearing them to steal the stolen pig's money. He is not the coy, persuasive trickster that the sandy whiskered gentleman is, and does not seek to persuade his victim to participate in his own fatal end. His amoral appropriation of Pigling Bland, without scruple as to how the pig appeared in the coop—"This one's come of himself, whatever" (46)—is compounded by his heartless imprisonment of Pig-Wig in the closet. His decision that Pigling "may sleep on the rug" (51), granted in an imperial tone, combined with his glance "at the small remains of a flitch" (51) of bacon, his consultation of an almanac, his examination of Pigling's ribs and his realization that the season is not right for slaughtering a pig, make him all the more designing.

His purposes are more than the simple motivation of a farmer to slaughter livestock for his own support. This farmer is apparently driven by profit, at the expense of other farmers and our hero. His threat to Pigling about tampering with his things while he is out—"I'll come back and skin ye!" (52)—seems likely to happen to Pigling anyway, even if Piperson disposes of him. His return in a "very affable" (59) mood, wherein he is generous with the porridge and forgets to secure both the meal chest and the closet door properly suggests that he is drunk, an inexcusable transgression upon propriety. This farmer has forfeited his farmer's right to the lives of the livestock for his own welfare. The stage is set for Pigling Bland and Pig-Wig to escape. Their destination is suggested in Tom the Piper's son's rhyme "But all the tune that he could play,/ was 'Over the hills and far away!'" (78).

Pigling's courtship of Pig-Wig begins with a touch of pathos overwhelmed by humor. He slips peppermints under the door to her in her closet-prison. These are "conversation mints" (24) of the kind that young gentlemen used in Victorian times both to woo young ladies and to suggest proper topics of conversation from the little sayings written in their wrapping paper. But there is no suggestion that Pigling talks to Pig-Wig during the day. Yet he does communicate, if only through the sentiments that accompany the mints.

When she is finally freed from the closet, Pig-Wig reveals herself as shallow but inveterately optimistic. Escape simply has not occured to her until Pigling suggests it. She knows that her fate is "Bacon, hams," but she answers Pigling "cheerfully" when he asked why she was stolen (63). When he suggests that she run away, she puts him off long enough to have her supper—a decision consistent with her pig nature, and one that Pigling himself makes when he decides to pay more attention to Piperson's dinner preparations than to "something at the further end of the kitchen" that "was taking a suppressed interest in the cooking" (48) when he first arrives. Thus, his stomach causes him to ignore Pig-Wig until he has satisfied his hunger.

Pig-Wig is willing, however thoughtlessly, to escape that night, but Pigling, who shows his canniness, suggests the wisdom of waiting till daylight. In spite of the danger posed by Piperson's presence in the bedroom, where he might waken either from the smell of the peppermints or from any noise, Pig-Wig sings herself to sleep, oblivious to the danger around her. Though she is not a thoughtful pig, yet she is an appropriate life's companion for Pigling and complements his talents and shortcomings. She knows the way out, but he knows the appropriate time to leave. He has a toothache, she has sympathy. He has the peppermints, but owing to this toothache, only she can eat them. She can run away, but only he can judge the appropriate moment to fool both Piperson and the grocer who threatens their happiness at the very last moment.

Their destination "over the hills and far away" (94), which can be arrived at only by crossing a bridge over which they cannot return, suggests the finality of the pigs' choice, both in running away and in doing so together. It also suggests Potter's own understanding of the change that both marriage and permanent residency in Sawrey would make in her life. Her vision of the rest of the world opening up in those distant hills, and the expansiveness of her landscape description in this book echo her love of the open landscape and her desire to make a small place in it for herself. The picture of Pig-wig and Pigling Bland dancing at the end of the book, with three rabbits looking on while they accompany the pigs on musical instruments, suggests a finality, a finished quality to the phase of Potter's life where rabbits and other small animals occupied her attention as author and illustrator.

Unlike her other books, *Pigling Bland* was not extended past its real ending. In fact, the reader is pleasantly, if somewhat abruptly surprised by the ending, since the eventual fate of the two pigs is only implied in the closing couplets arranged as prose: "They came to the river, they came to the bridge—they crossed it hand in hand—then over the hills and far away she danced with Pigling Bland!" (93–94). There is no description of their occupations in later life, as with Ginger and Pickles or Tom Kitten and sisters or Jemima Puddle-Duck. The book's end comes as a surprise because of the heightened tension in the lines preceding, underscored by the nearly breathless rhythm of the sentences. The tension is further drawn out because the two halves of the ending rhyme are separated by a turn of the page, and the fact that the rhyme is a rhyme at all is not clear until the "Pigling Bland" is made to rhyme with "hand in hand." The neat ending in couplet suggests a Shakespearean influence, as does the final dance, in its reassertion of cosmic order and continuance of life. The presence of the signpost, both in the frontispiece and in the final picture, suggests that the turning point is a clear, conscious decision to choose happiness and the farmer's way of life for Potter. The musical accompaniment by the rabbits signals a career come full circle, with the rabbits of the earlier books joining the pigs in a grand finale.

Potter's pictures for the story show her growing predilection for pen-and-ink sketches, and the felicity she felt resulted from quick sketching rather than laborious drawing. Certainly her drawings of the humans so prominent in this story was aided by this rapid method of composition, and by her good sense in focusing more on the animals in the story rather than on the humans. Her pictures of herself, at first just as a hand helping to dress the pigs for market, then in full frontal pose, are happily posed, in that she does not give her own figure facial detail, and the lack of eyes makes her presence less obtrusive. The presence of the hand is metaphorically suggestive, in that she is lending Aunt Pettitoes a hand in raising the litter, and in that she has a hand in deciding the piglets' fates. Warne's method of producing her books had changed, so that the colored pictures could not be placed anywhere in the book but only at designated intervals. Yet Potter was careful not to set what she considered too much text opposite the pictures, and carefully coordinated each picture opposite the appropriate text. This was the last time that she would take such care with a book, preparing more than a few colored drawings and creating a whole new story.

Chapter Five

The Potter Industry

For all that she tried to protect herself against fame and public invasion of her privacy, Beatrix Potter knew that her books would someday be nursery classics. In her old age she remarked to a cousin-by-marriage, Ulla Hyde Parker, that she fully expected her books to be as popular and as well-read as Hans Christian Andersen's fairy tales.[1] Though the assertion may have sounded like boasting at the time, even her cousin understood the confidence and self-assurance that making such a statement implies; and, indeed, Potter's evaluation of her own work has proven true.

Part of the longevity of her books comes from marketing strategy. Potter was never averse to the nonliterary uses of her books as long as they did not violate copyright. In fact, she herself invented toy letters for the Moore children, with flaps that moved up and down revealing pop-up rabbits and other animals. That her books should inspire toys did not offend her. Her main objection to the many stuffed toys fashioned after her characters soon after they appeared in print was that she derived no economic benefit from them. The loss of artistic control, as with poorly executed toys or books bowdlerized in text or re-illustrated by other artists, was less important than the money that she lost when international copyright laws failed to protect her. This is not to say that her only concern was for the money her books brought her. Rather, it points to what the money stood for: recognition of her hard work and achievement, the fact that she could do something with her life worthy of public recognition. The theft of her work meant the theft of her worth as an artist. Though after her marriage much of her self-confidence derived from her status as wife, successful farmer, and landowner, yet she never relinquished her sense of achievement in her writing and art.

Potter certainly encouraged these nonliterary uses of her books, and one need not look far to find the result: Peter Rabbit pencil boxes, figurines, Christmas ornaments, board games, even dish towels. For the most part, the reproductions are well done and apparently profitable. For example, Wedgewood has a line of nursery dishes, with the

Peter Rabbit story reproduced on teacups, cereal bowls, plates, and coin banks. It must be a worthwhile line of products or Royal Doulton, a competing china company, would not have brought out a line of figurines and nursery dishes, with animals similar to Potter's but not exactly the same.

Her pictures are the source of much of the commercial use of her books, but her words and story lines have also found perpetuation in other sources than print. *The Beatrix Potter Ballet,* staged and filmed by EMI Productions of London in 1971, sought to incorporate most of Potter's most famous characters and story lines into one continuous dramatic presentation. In 1923 E. Harcourt Williams adapted *The Tailor of Gloucester* into a children's play, and Potter consented to its publication with the proviso that she be allowed to revise it before publication. In 1931 Potter and Williams continued their collaboration with a dramatized version of *Ginger and Pickles,* and in 1933 Theron H. Butterworth dramatized and published his version of *Mr. Samuel Whiskers*—the English title of *The Roly-Poly Pudding.* In 1967 Christopher Le Fleming composed music for Potter's own dramatic adaptation of *Squirrel Nutkin* and published it under the title *Squirrel Nutkin, A Children's Play Adapted by Beatrix Potter from her original story, Music adapted from traditional tunes by Christopher Le Fleming.*[2] Le Fleming had written the music for *The Peter Rabbit Music Books* (1935), for which Potter had provided some preliminary pencil drawings.

Her own adaptation, with newly executed drawings and shortening of text, of *Peter Rabbit, Tom Kitten,* and *Jemima Puddle-Duck* into painting books in 1911, 1917, and 1925, show her willingness to market her books and change their formats to cash in on their commercial possibilities. The publisher's note on the inside cover indicates the use of one publication to promote another: "These outline pictures for you to colour are all from Beatrix Potter's Peter Rabbit books. You might like to read the stories after you have painted the pictures. A full list appears on the back cover."[3] Dover has brought out in this country a coloring book based on *Peter Rabbit,* but the pictures are much less satisfactory than Potter's own, given that the fine lines of her drawing look unsure, spindly, and busy as redrawn for a full-sized page by Nancy Perkins.[4]

Potter's Popularity

Part of the reason that these other products sell at all is the enduring popularity of Potter's books. The manifestations of Potter's art in its other commercial forms would not exist were it not for tie-ins with the books. But the books themselves are sometimes less satisfactory in reproduction than are the subsequent permutations of Potter's art into products. The original plates for Potter's books have deteriorated; the colors and fine lines in issues now available do not compare with those of the original editions. The pictures are sometimes blurred, and the vividness of the colors compromised. The diminished size of some of the books originally designed for a large format has weakened the overall effect.

The seventy-fifth anniversary of the publication of *Peter Rabbit* was the occasion for Potter's publisher to market the whole Peter Rabbit series and to promote commercial spinoffs of the books. These Potter products for children spring from the nostalgia about childhood that has existed since Victorian times. Adults turn to children's books that were favorites when they themselves were young and buy them for their child acquaintances. Adults may remember the stories only incompletely, however, with unpleasant incidents and reactions conveniently forgotten. Thus, the first generation to enjoy the unique achievement of Potter's creations enshrined her works. The American "professional priestesses of 'kid. lit.,'" as Margaret Lane has called them,[5] added their imprimatur to Potter's image, and helped foster her reputation on both sides of the Atlantic. The Potter books are now a traditional part of childhood in most English-speaking countries and in many of the countries into whose languages Potter's books have been translated. Raising children is, except in rare instances, a conservative activity; part of the experience that is conserved is the work of Beatrix Potter and the assumption that most children will like her books. This is not to say that Potter's books are not suitable, but only that buyers have remained uncritical.

Since the time of Aesop's fables, animals and stories about them have been assumed to be appropriate vehicles for moral messages. The transformation of the beast fable into the children's story was an easy leap, especially in the eighteenth century, when moral education became a primary goal. As rural landscape gave way to urban settings and the problems in the industrial revolution, the life of country and farm, including animal inhabitants, gradually became idealized. Thus, the nostalgia for childhood gradually incorporated idealization of farm and wild animals.

The environmental conservation movement beginning in the early twentieth century and the inculcation of its values among children added to the new interest in wildlife studies and animal stories for the young. Potter's books appeared at a time when animals and their lives were a ritual and requisite part of any young child's education. As Margaret Blount says, animal books are the kind that adults enjoy giving to children, regardless of whether children truly enjoy reading them.[6]

Potter's books are particularly enjoyable for adults to read because of her subtle humor and lack of condescension, especially when the pictures comment ironically about the action and when the language is elegant. As Patricia Dooley has noted, when a parent can expect to read the same book over and over to please a child, anything the least bit interesting to the adult can be a welcome relief to the tedium. And as she further notes, the favorites of the adult rapidly become the favorites of the child.[7] Especially in the mouse books, the detail of the pictures can supply new items of interest in repeated readings, another source of relief for the adult.

For the child, the pictures supply what Diana Klemin has called a "common visual heritage,"[8] showing how Western culture assumes that rabbit, mice, gardens, and country landscape should look. Picture books for the very young also introduce the child to the book itself and the conventions of reading. For example, children learn by experiences with books that books open with the binding to the left and continue chronologically from front to back. The pictures correspond in some way to the text on the same page or double-page spread. But though pictures and text may appear on the same page, the letters of the words are not part of the picture, even though the words may appear superimposed. The turning of pages indicates the passage of time. Pictures of the same characters appear and denote the same characters, not different ones, even though they may appear on different pages. All of these are conventions that children are not born with, but rather come to understand as they experience books, especially early picture books, including Potter's.

Because the Potter books are small, they do not adapt well to large storytelling situations, where many children might try to look at the same pictures at the same time. But their diminutive size does encourage an intimacy between adult reader and child listener, or between the child and the book. This experience of intimacy, between adult and child, and between the child and the easily handled book, encourages a comfortable, enjoying attitude toward reading, which was certainly in Potter's mind when she designed the small format. The relatively inexpensive price—as Potter said, all her young readers were "shilling" people"[9]—and the excellent quality of paper and binding even today, ensure a book that is both durable and important-feeling, the fine paper giving a sense of permanency and significance to the story and pleasure to the tactile aspects of the reading experience. One cannot overlook the relevance of the "feel" of a book in encouraging children to enjoy the reading. Books that smack of ephemerality and a trivial, "throw-away" experience may make for passing reading pleasure but give little sense of the dignity and durability of the joy of reading. Even the typeface may add to the reading experience. In Potter's case the type is a simple Roman style, but the added width of the downstrokes underscores the density and solidness of her blocks of text, while the small serifs lend a sense of elegance to her words. All of these features of her books tend to enhance their popularity.

Critical Appraisal

Most of the discussion thus far of Potter's popularity has dealt with issues unrelated to the genuine quality of her books. Granted, children and the buyers and purveyors of children's books are not infallible critics of children's literature, but in the case of Beatrix Potter their confidence in the quality of her books has not been misplaced. The books have thriven in translation into several different languages and have persisted as favorites through several generations of youthful readers. The books, *Peter Rabbit* especially, have been retold, re-illustrated, and otherwise violated by other authors and illustrators. Yet the originals endure, not to be overtaken by more modern updatings.

One of the reasons for this remarkable longevity is Potter's unwillingness to compromise the truth in order to shelter young readers. Though her endings are happy ones, they do not deny the existence of pain and death, and do not skirt the enmity between various animal species, or between the animals and human beings. Big animals eat little animals; humans eat all kinds of creatures. Adults sometimes use language that children do not quite understand, the meaning of which they can still derive from context. But though she does not deal with the more mature, bloody, grisly aspects of carnivore life, Potter faces it, admits it, and yet does not terrorize children with it. Her animals, especially the rabbits, glance fearfully out at the reader, as if admitting the frank terror with which human presence inspires them. As Blount says, the stories and pictures give credence to the idea that Potter is telling the truth, that the stories might really have happened, but never in the presence of human beings.[10] Thus, the reader is invited into the fantasy with a sense that he is not being patronized, and that life is not being edited for his benefit and protection.

The animals are all small, and with the exception of the frogs, ducks, and insects, are all mammals, if not always furry and pettable, as with the hedgehogs and pigs. But their smallness makes them "rubbish" as Potter called them,[11] all expendable animals, not those who work for a living, such as horses and sheepdogs. The smallness here is important; they are all smaller than children and thus inspire childlike mastery and patronage of their smallness. None of the animals is the equal of a child either in intelligence or size, and thus each can be admired by a child or sympathetic adult without being dealt with as a creature of equal or greater power or stature. The furry animals particularly invite sympathy because of the pleasure of petting them. But even Mrs. Tiggy and Pigling Bland have their charming, admirable qualities that make them pets rather than livestock. Jemima Puddle-Duck is the only central character who might be considered a "working" animal; but her unreliable nerves make her attempts at labor humorous, and she is too unsteady to be a producer of eggs and ducklings in the manner of a reliable farm duck. The piglets are surplus, and not yet large enough to be livestock; they are sent to market rather than being kept on the farm to be seriously businesslike. Thus their expendability and youthfulness makes them pets as well.

Potter's popularity has influenced her followers, but her influence is not as obvious among writers as it is among illustrators. Almost all rabbits in children's stories now look like Peter, and almost all landscapes are as expansively drawn and extensively colored. Though, as Margaret Blount points out, Potter's landscapes are of real places,[12] yet for modern readers they are also idealized, for though the unspoiled Lake District still exists, it is not familiar to all readers, and most landscapes are somehow marred by the years intervening since Potter drew hers. The virgin territory that Potter recorded is almost unknown in technologically advanced cultures, as is the simple country life she preserved, especially in the Sawrey books. As in her work for the National Trust, one of Potter's greatest legacies is her preservation, both in the lands held in trust and in her books, of the way of life she came to live in that isolated part of England. This idealization of a landscape and a lifestyle now archaic, but also actually experienced, is part of the nostalgic, Anglophilic domain that predominates in illustrating for children.

Most of Potter's followers in the genre of the animal story are not really heirs to her legacy, for they follow the habits of Leslie Brooke and Thornton Burgess in giving animals clothing and personifying them without remaining true to animal nature. In many ways these animals are simply humans with animal heads on their shoulders, tricked out in elaborate but functionless human accessories. Though Marcus Crouch points to Alison Uttley and her Grey Rabbit books as direct heirs of Potter's animal techniques, yet these animals also do not wear their clothes as comfortably as do Peter Rabbit and kin. The heritage lies more clearly, as Crouch says, in the love of country life rather than in the actualization of animalness in Uttley's creations.[13] As mentioned above, Potter is part of the trend in idealizing rural life as the perfect locale for childhood, but it is more the trend than Potter's direct influence that persists.

In the realm of bookmaking her influence is much clearer. Her format has been borrowed by a number of publishing houses for series of books, mostly of the inexpensive, easily reproduced sort. Some illustrators have tried re-illustrating Potter's books. But for an artist to take on the project of retelling a story where the illustrations are so well known that they are virtually identified as the story, where illustration and story are so familiar and intertwined as to be inseparable, the illustrator must have a whole new vision of the story, something new to say about it in his illustrations. That new vision must be clearly bodied forth in his illustrations so that the story really becomes his own. Few artists have tried and even fewer have succeeded in this task, and none have managed to do anything with Potter's books other than to disrupt and misinterpret the tales.

Potter's use of color and exquisite detail set a new standard in color illustration for children's books, and encouraged the use of more color and more careful drafting in pictures. Though it is difficult to single out any particular authors and illustrators who followed Potter as direct heirs, it is easy to see the greater attention to color, especially watercolor, and detail, and the increased number of serious artists who found children's books an appropriate medium for their professional efforts. Potter still maintains this standard for children's books and is not likely to be replaced or surpassed any time soon.

Potter's animals are all true to life, both as animals and as fictional characters. The reactions of her child readers kept Potter honest, both to child nature and to animal nature. The stories seem as if they might have happened. They do not beg questions to interrupt the feeling of internal consistency in the conception of the fantasy, the pursuit of the answers to which might have interrupted the suspension of disbelief that makes their fantasy possible. If one has not seen such animals, it is because they do not live in close, intimate quarter with human beings, or perhaps because one is not attentive enough. Only Potter could see what these animals were doing, and through her patient, carefully chronicled stories we come to know what J. R. R. Tolkien said is one of the most fervent wishes of humankind: to know what animals are actually saying.[14] Potter's stories answer for the reader not only what animals are like, but also function as fairy tales do in telling us human beings what we are like. In her criticism of human manners and society Potter openly attacks human prejudice and presumption, and yet by using animals as her vehicles of criticism, she also shows the way to human improvement: be like animals, honest, straightforward, even violent, but always truthful and true to nature.

Notes and References

Chapter One

1. Leslie Linder, *A History of the Writings of Beatrix Potter: Including Unpublished Work* (London and New York, 1971), 158; hereafter cited as Linder, *Writings of BP*.
2. 11 July 1895, *The Journal of Beatrix Potter*, ed. Leslie Linder (London and New York, 1966), 381; hereafter page references cited in parentheses in the text.
3. Margaret Lane, *The Magic Years of Beatrix Potter* (London and New York, 1978), 200.
4. Linder, *Writings of BP*, xxv.
5. *The History of the Tale of Peter Rabbit: Taken mainly from Leslie Linder's "A History of the Writings of Beatrix Potter": Together with the Text and Illustrations from the First Privately Printed Edition* (London and New York, 1976). 11.
6. Ulla Hyde Parker, *Cousin Beatie: A Memory of Beatrix Potter* (London, 1981), 30, 32.
7. Arthur King and A. F. Stuart, *The House of Warne: One Hundred Years of Publishing* (London and New York: Frederick Warne, 1965), 10.
8. Lane, *Magic Years*, 21.
9. H. L. Cox, in "An Appreciation," *Journal of Beatrix Potter*, xviii.
10. Linder, *Writings of BP*, 184.
11. Margaret Lane, *The Tale of Beatrix Potter*, rev. ed. (N. p.: Fontana/Collins Books, 1970), 125; hereafter cited as Lane, *Tale of BP*.
12. Roger Sale, "Beatrix Potter," Chapter 6 in *Fairy Tales and After: From Snow White to E. B. White* (Cambridge, Mass. and London, 1978), 135.

Chapter Two

1. Joel Chandler Harris, *Uncle Remus*, introduction by Stella Brewer Brookes (1880; reprint, New York: Schocken, 1965), 7.
2. *The Tale of Peter Rabbit* (New York, [1902]), 42; hereafter page references cited in parentheses in the text.
3. *The History of the Tale of Peter Rabbit*, 11; further references cited as H followed by page number in the text.
4. Linder, *Writings of BP*, 96.
5. Ibid.
6. Ibid.
7. Ibid., 264.

8. Grahame Greene, "Beatrix Potter," in *Collected Essays* (New York, 1969), 235.

9. *The Tale of Benjamin Bunny* (New York, 1904), 25; hereafter page references cited in parentheses in the text.

10. Linder, *Writings of BP,* 146.

11. Ibid.

12. Ibid.

13. Ibid., 146–47.

14. Ibid., 144.

15. Ibid., 145.

16. Leslie Linder and Enid Linder, eds., *The Art of Beatrix Potter: With an Appreciation by Anne Carroll Moore,* rev. ed. (New York and London, 1972), 337.

17. *The Tale of the Flopsy Bunnies* (New York, 1909), 10; hereafter page references cited in parentheses in the text.

18. Lane, *Magic Years,* 173.

19. Linder, *Writings of BP,* 211.

20. *The Tale of Mr. Tod* (New York, 1912), 7; hereafter page references cited in parentheses in the text.

21. Linder, *Writings of BP,* 211.

22. Ibid., 210.

23. Lane, *Magic Years,* 189.

24. Linder, *Writings of BP,* 210.

25. Celia Catlett Anderson, "The Ancient Lineage of Beatrix Potter's Mr. Tod," in *Festschrift: A Ten Year Retrospective,* ed. Perry Nodelman and Jill P. May (West Lafayette, Ind., 1983), 45–46.

26. Ibid., 46.

27. Ibid., 46–47.

28. *The Story of a Fierce Bad Rabbit* (New York, 1906), 9; hereafter page references cited in parentheses in the text.

Chapter Three

1. Lane, *Tale of BP,* 154.

2. *The Tailor of Gloucester* (New York, 1903), 9: hereafter page references cited in parentheses in the text.

3. Linder, *Writings of BP,* 112.

4. *The Tailor of Gloucester: From the Original Manuscript* (London and New York, 1968), 16; hereafter cited in the text as *O* followed by page number.

5. Linder, *Writings of BP,* 125.

6. Ibid., 116.

7. Ibid., 133.

8. Ibid., 134.

9. Ibid., 125.
10. Ibid., 120.
11. Ibid., 135.
12. *The Tale of Squirrel Nutkin* (New York, 1903), 18; hereafter page references cited in parentheses in the text.
13. Lane, *Tale of BP,* 91.
14. *The Tale of Two Bad Mice* (New York, 1904), 13; hereafter page references cited in parentheses in the text.
15. Margaret Blount, *Animal Land: The Creatures of Children's Fiction* (New York, 1975), 142.
16. Linder, *Writings of BP,* 152.
17. Ibid.
18. Lane, *Magic Years,* 185.
19. *The Tale of Timmy Tiptoes* (New York, 1911), 22; hereafter page references cited in parentheses in the text.
20. *The Tale of Johnny Town-Mouse* (New York, 1918), 59.
21. *The Tale of Little Pig Robinson* (New York, 1930), 22.

Chapter Four

1. Roger Sale, "Beatrix Potter," 142.
2. *The Tale of Mrs. Tiggy-Winkle* (New York, 1905), 25; hereafter page references cited in parentheses in the text.
3. Linder, *Writings of BP,* 156.
4. *The Tale of the Pie and the Patty-Pan* (New York, 1905). 8; hereafter page references cited in parentheses in the text.
5. Marcus Crouch, *Beatrix Potter; A Walck Monograph* (New York, 1961), 38.
6. *The Tale of Tom Kitten* (New York, 1907), 18; hereafter page references cited in parentheses in the text.
7. *The Roly-Poly Pudding* (New York, 1908), 53; hereafter page references cited in parentheses in the text.
8. Linder, *Writings of BP,* 192.
9. Lane, *Magic Years,* 160.
10. Greene, "Beatrix Potter," 239.
11. Linder, *Writings of BP,* 193.
12. Lane, *Magic Years,* 173.
13. Ibid., 155.
14. *The Tale of Jemima Puddle-Duck* (New York, 1908), 22; hereafter page references cited in parentheses in the text.
15. Lane, *Magic Years,* 157.
16. Greene, "Beatrix Potter," 236.
17. *Ginger and Pickles* (New York, 1909), 19–20; hereafter page references cited in parentheses in the text.

18. Linder, *Writings of BP,* 205.

19. *The Tale of Pigling Bland* (New York, 1913), 94; hereafter page references cited in parentheses in the text.

20. Linder, *Writings of BP,* 213.

21. William S. Baring-Gould and Ceil Baring-Gould, *The Annotated Mother Goose: Nursery Rhymes Old and New, Arranged and Explained* (New York: Bramhall House, 1962), 231.

Chapter Five

1. Parker, *Cousin Beatie,* 23.

2. Linder, *Writings of BP,* 276.

3. *Beatrix Potter's Painting Book 2: Outline Pictures from the Peter Rabbit books* (London and New York: Frederick Warne, 1978).

4. Beatrix Potter, *The Tale of Peter Rabbit by Beatrix Potter: A Coloring Book,* rendered for coloring by Nancy Perkins (New York: Dover, 1971).

5. Lane, *Magic Years,* 200.

6. Blount, *Animal Land,* 15.

7. Patricia Dooley, "'First Books': From Schlock to Sophistication," in *Festschrift: A Ten Year Retrospective,* ed. Perry Nodelman and Jill P. May (West Lafayette, Ind., 1983), 41–43.

8. Diana Klemin, *The Illustrated Book: Its Art and Craft* (New York: Clarkson Potter, 1970), 18.

9. Linder, *Writings of BP,* 142.

10. Blount, *Animal Land,* 28, 136, 138.

11. Lane, *Tale of BP,* 154.

12. Blount, *Animal Land,* 156.

13. Crouch, *Beatrix Potter,* 60.

14. J. R. R. Tolkien, "On Fairy Stories" in *The Tolkien Reader,* introduction by Peter S. Beagle (New York: Ballantine Books, 1966), 84.

Selected Bibliography

PRIMARY SOURCES

1. The Peter Rabbit series
The Tale of Peter Rabbit. New York: Frederick Warne [1902].
The Tailor of Gloucester. New York: Frederick Warne, 1903.
The Tale of Squirrel Nutkin. New York: Frederick Warne, 1903.
The Tale of Benjamin Bunny. New York: Frederick Warne, 1904.
The Tale of Two Bad Mice. New York: Frederick Warne, 1904.
The Tale of Mrs. Tiggy-Winkle. New York: Frederick Warne, 1905.
The Tale of the Pie and the Patty-Pan. New York: Frederick Warne, 1905.
The Story of a Fierce Bad Rabbit. New York: Frederick Warne, 1906.
The Story of Miss Moppet. New York: Frederick Warne, 1906.
The Tale of Mr. Jeremy Fisher. New York: Frederick Warne, 1906.
The Tale of Tom Kitten. New York: Frederick Warne, 1907.
The Tale of Jemima Puddle-Duck. New York: Frederick Warne, 1908.
The Roly-Poly Pudding. New York: Frederick Warne, 1908.
The Tale of the Flopsy Bunnies. New York: Frederick Warne, 1909.
Ginger and Pickles. New York: Frederick Warne, 1909.
The Tale of Mrs. Tittlemouse. New York: Frederick Warne, 1910.
The Tale of Timmy Tiptoes. New York: Frederick Warne, 1911.
The Tale of Mr. Tod. New York: Frederick Warne, 1912.
The Tale of Pigling Bland. New York: Frederick Warne, 1913.
Appley Dapply's Nursery Rhymes. New York: Frederick Warne, 1917.
The Tale of Johnny Town-Mouse. New York: Frederick Warne, 1918.
Cecily Parsley's Nursery Rhymes. New York: Frederick Warne, 1922.
The Tale of Little Pig Robinson. New York: Fredeick Warne, 1930.

2. Other
Beatrix Potter's Americans: Selected Letters. Edited by Jane Crowell Morse. Boston: The Horn Book, 1982.
The Fairy Caravan. Philadelphia: David McKay, 1929; new edition, London and New York: Frederick Warne, 1952.
Findlay, W. P. K. *Wayside and Woodland Fungi.* Illustrated by Beatrix Potter. London and New York: Frederick Warne, 1967.

A Frog He Would a-Fishing Go. Illustrated by Beatrix Potter. London: Ernest
   Nister, and New York: E. P. Dutton [1895].
Jemima Puddle-Duck's Painting Book. London and New York: Frederick Warne,
   1925.
The Journal of Beatrix Potter from 1881 to 1897. Edited and transcribed by
   Leslie Linder. London and New York: Frederick Warne, 1966.
Letters to Children. Cambridge, Mass.: Harvard College Library, Department
   of Printing and Graphic Arts; New York: Walker, 1966.
"On the Germination of the Spores of *Agaricineae.*" Presented to the Linnaean
   Society, London, 1 April 1897.
Peter Rabbit's Almanac for 1929. London: Frederick Warne, 1928.
Peter Rabbit's Painting Book. London: Frederick Warne, 1911.
Sister Anne. Philadelphia: David MacKay, 1932.
The Sly Old Cat. London and New York: Frederick Warne, 1971.
"The Strength that Comes from the Hills: From a Letter of Beatrix Potter's
   to *The Horn Book,* Early in 1941." *Horn Book* 20 (1944):77.
The Tailor of Gloucester: From the Original Manuscript. London and New York:
   Frederick Warne, 1968.
The Tale of the Faithful Dove. Illustrated by Marie Angell. London and New
   York: Frederick Warne, 1955.
The Tale of Tuppenny. Illustrated by Marie Angell. London and New York:
   Frederick Warne, 1973.
Tom Kitten's Painting Book. London: Frederick Warne, 1917.
Wag-by-Wall. Boston: The Horn Book, 1944.
Weatherly, Frederic. *A Happy Pair.* Illustrated by Beatrix Potter. London:
   Ernest Nister, 1890.

SECONDARY SOURCES

1. Biographies
Lane, Margaret. *The Magic Years of Beatrix Potter.* London and New York:
   Frederick Warne, 1978. A revision, including new materials, especially
   Potter's journal, of Lane's earlier definitive biography.
————. *The Tale of Beatrix Potter.* Rev. ed. N. p.: Fontana/Collins Books,
   1970. The definitive biography of Potter, locating her source of creativ-
   ity in her prolonged adolescence.

2. Books, Parts of Books, and Articles
Anderson, Celia Catlett. "The Ancient Lineage of Beatrix Potter's Mr. Tod."
   In *Festschrift: A Ten Year Retrospective.* Edited by Perry Nodelman and Jill

P. May, 45–47. West Lafayette, Ind.: Children's Literature Association Publications, 1983. A comparison of Mr. Tod to Reynard and to foxes in Aesop's fables.

Banner, Delmar. "Memories of Beatrix Potter." *Nineteenth Century and After* 140 (October 1946):230–32. A personal reminiscence about Potter from the painter of her portrait; evaluates her personality in the years after her publishing period.

Blount, Margaret. *Animal Land: The Creatures of Children's Fiction*. New York: William Morrow, 1975. Mentions of Potter throughout; particularly strong in locating the appeal of various species of animals used in Potter's stories and in examining her creation of a fantasy world in a real setting.

Boultbee, Winifred. "Some Personal Recollections of Beatrix Potter." *Horn Book* 47 (1971):586–88. Written by the owner of the dollhouse featured in *The Tale of Two Bad Mice,* remembering her reactions to Potter when Boultbee was a child. Of importance in clarifying children's reactions to Potter during her publishing period.

Crouch, Marcus. *Beatrix Potter: A Walck Monograph*. New York: Henry Z. Walck, 1961. The definitive work on Potter's writing, this evaluates the books in terms of their connections to the author's own life.

Eastman, Jackie F. "Elements of *The Tale of Peter Rabbit:* Proportion, Plot, and Peter Himself". In *Touchstones of Children's Literature,* edited by Perry Nodelman, 45–52. West Lafayette, Ind.: Children's Literature Association Publications, 1985. Attributes the success of the story to its unity of proportion, simplicity, dramatic tension, and unique appeal of the hero.

Gilpatrick, Naomi. "Secret Life of Beatrix Potter." *Natural History* 81:38–41, ff. Traces Potter's development in her research on fungi.

Godden, Rumer. "An Imaginary Correspondence." *Horn Book* 39 (1963):369–75. A hypothetical examination of the unthinkable: the re-telling and re-illustration of Potter's books according to modern educational ideas and publishing practices.

————. "Beatrix Potter." *Horn Book* 42 (1966):390–98. A centenary essay tracing the popularity of Potter's books and her superior achievement in language and handling of details in the books.

————. *The Tale of Tales: The Beatrix Potter Ballet*. New York and London: Frederick Warne, 1971. An insider's view of the production of the ballet, from its inception to its final filming.

Greene, Grahame. "Beatrix Potter." In *Collected Essays,* 232–40. New York: Viking, 1969. Important for its overview of Potter's entire career and its analysis of the change in tone and complexity in the books in the final years of her publishing period.

Hearn, Michael Patrick. "A Second Look: Peter Rabbit Redux." *Horn Book* 53 (1977):563–66. Examines the longevity of *Peter Rabbit* and finds reasons for it in the details about food and in Potter's construction of the narrative.

Lanes, Selma G. *Down the Rabbit Hole: Adventures and Misadventures in the Realm of Children's Literature.* New York: Atheneum, 1971. Mentions of Potter throughout; an examination of the appeal of Potter's books to children and children's particular attention to Potter's rabbits and mice.

Linder, Leslie, ed. *The History of the Tale of Peter Rabbit. Taken mainly from Leslie Linder's "A History of the Writings of Beatrix Potter": Together with the Text and Illustrations from the First Privately Printed Edition.* London and New York: Frederick Warne, 1976. Important for its inclusion of the original picture letter and for the complete text of the first edition. Some illustrations deleted at various times in the book's history are also included.

————. *A History of the Writings of Beatrix Potter: Including Unpublished Works.* London and New York: Frederick Warne, 1971. A careful cataloging of all Potter's works, both published and unpublished, and a consideration of all her correspondence with her publishers.

———— and **Enid Linder**, eds. *The Art of Beatrix Potter: With an Appreciation by Anne Carroll Moore and Notes to each Section by Enid and Leslie Linder.* Rev. ed. London and New York: Frederick Warne, 1972. Reproductions and overview of all of Potter's artwork throughout her life, both in her books and in her portfolios.

"Menander's Mirror." *Times Literary Supplement,* 8 January 1944, 15. At her death, evaluating Potter's popularity because of the books' lack of moralities and their noneducational bent. Also praises Potter for her factual style of fantasy and her traditional plotting techniques.

Miller, Bertha M. "Beatrix Potter in Letters." *Horn Book* 20 (1944):214–24. A history of the correspondence between Potter and Miller, leading to the publication of Potter's letters and stories in the *Horn Book.*

Parker, Ulla Hyde. *Cousin Beatie: A Memory of Beatrix Potter.* London: Frederick Warne, 1981. A personal recollection from a distant cousin by marriage, remarkable for its insight into Potter's relationship with her neighbors and with children.

Rolland, Deborah. *Beatrix Potter in Scotland.* London: Frederick Warne, 1981. An examination of Potter's Scottish vacations and their inspiration for her books.

"'Roots' of the Peter Rabbit Tales." *Horn Book* 5(1929):69–72. Potter's own explanation of her sources of inspiration for the rabbit-bunny books.

Sale, Roger. "Beatrix Potter." Chapter 6 in *Fairy Tales and After: From Snow White to E. B. White.* Cambridge, Mass., and London: Harvard University Press, 1978. A thorough examination of all of Potter's books, with an understanding of her love of the small, her creation of horror, and her development of atmosphere and focus in her pictures.

Sendak, Maurice. "Aliveness of Peter Rabbit." *Wilson Library Bulletin* 40 (1965):345–48. Finds longevity in Potter's book in its tone of conviction and in the blend of fantasy and realism.

Slowe, V. A. J. *The Art of Beatrix Potter.* Kendal, United Kingdom: Abbot Hall Art Gallery, n. d. Written for an exhibition at the gallery of Potter's works, and particularly noteworthy for its history of her studies of fungi.

Index